Strengthening Analytics in Mexico's Supreme Audit Institution

CONSIDERATIONS AND PRIORITIES FOR ASSESSING INTEGRITY RISKS

This document, as well as any data and map included herein, are without prejudice to the status of or sovereignty over any territory, to the delimitation of international frontiers and boundaries and to the name of any territory, city or area.

Please cite this publication as:
OECD (2022), *Strengthening Analytics in Mexico's Supreme Audit Institution: Considerations and Priorities for Assessing Integrity Risks*, OECD Public Governance Reviews, OECD Publishing, Paris, https://doi.org/10.1787/d4f685b7-en.

ISBN 978-92-64-65067-1 (print)
ISBN 978-92-64-55388-0 (pdf)
ISBN 978-92-64-90110-0 (HTML)
ISBN 978-92-64-73419-7 (epub)

OECD Public Governance Reviews
ISSN 2219-0406 (print)
ISSN 2219-0414 (online)

Foreword

The Supreme Audit Institution (SAI) of Mexico, the Superior Audit of the Federation, (*Auditoría Superior de la Federación*, or ASF) is one of the best institutional examples of Mexico's commitment to digital transformation. Its efforts align, and in many ways are ahead of, various national plans and broader trends in Mexico to build a system of digital government. These trends include the government-wide initiatives of the Office for Coordination of the National Digital Strategy, within the Office of the President, as well as the Ministry of Public Administration. In the accountability and integrity domain, the digital trends are also visible in the strategies and efforts of the National Anti-Corruption System (*Sistema Nacional Anticorrupción*, NACS), which leads the development of the National Digital Platform (*Plataforma Digital Nacional*, PDN) to support NACS members with new technologies, methodologies, data science and artificial intelligence.

The ASF plays a key role in steering the NACS as well as the National Auditing System (*Sistema Nacional de Fiscalización,* NAS). As such, the success of the ASF's own digital transformation is tied to these broader systems. The ASF's work programme for digital transformation reflects the leadership's commitment to providing its auditors with the tools and skills needed to effectively hold government actors accountable in the modern era. Like many SAIs, investment in the infrastructure, architecture, databases and capacity to facilitate the work of auditors has become an even greater imperative for the ASF in the wake of the COVID-19 pandemic. On the one hand, this context brought new challenges for auditors, such as remote auditing as well as the need for more effective and efficient identification of risks stemming from economic stimulus. On the other hand, it has inspired new solutions, including innovations around digitalisation, data and analytics for safeguarding integrity.

To support these solutions, the OECD reviewed the ASF's use of analytics for detecting integrity risks, building on previous recommendations made in the 2017 *Mexico's National Auditing System: Strengthening Accountable Governance* report and the subsequent 2021 *Progress Report on the Implementation of the Mexican Superior Audit of the Federation's Mandate* report.

This report takes a deeper look at these issues with a focus on integrity risks and the ASF's strategies and efforts to integrate data and analytics into its operations. The report draws from the OECD's body of work to support governments in designing and implementing risk-based strategies and tools to strengthen accountability and safeguard integrity, as emphasised in the *OECD Recommendation on Public Integrity*. On a practical level, data and analytics are critical ingredients for achieving a risk-based approach, which for the ASF have implications both internally and for the institutions it oversees.

The scope of the report reflects the ASF's priority to invest in its own digital transformation, as well as a self-awareness about how it can enhance its oversight. While it focuses on the integrity context, the report recognises that improvements in one area of data or analytics, such as detecting fraud or corruption risks, matter for other data-driven applications and even for the ASF's broader strategy. Recommendations in this report take this into account, covering a range of strategic and operational considerations for ASF to improve the use of data and analytics.

This report was produced under the leadership of Elsa Pilichowski, Director, OECD Public Governance Directorate; János Bertók, Deputy Director for Public Governance; and Julio Bacio Terracino, Head of the Public Sector Integrity Division (PSI). The report was drafted by Gavin Ugale, Policy Advisor in PSI, with important contributions from Jacobo Pastor García Villarreal and Varun Banthia. Meral Gedik supported editing and formatting, and Charles Victor provided administrative assistance.

The report builds on nearly a decade of collaboration between the OECD and the ASF. The OECD would like to thank ASF for its fruitful co-operation and leadership. In particular, the OECD would like to thank David Colmenares Páramo, Supreme Auditor; Eber Betanzos, Technical Secretariat; Claudia María Bazúa, Financial Compliance Special Auditor; and Emilio Barriga Delgado, Federalised Spending Special Auditor; as well as their teams. Soo Jung Koh Yoo, Director for Multilateral Relations, in the ASF Technical Secretariat Office, served as the contact point for the project.

The OECD is also grateful to the peer experts who participated in a workshop on data analytics, jointly organised with ASF and held on 17-19 November 2020, including the General Comptroller's Office of Peru, the National Audit Office of Finland and the UK Government Digital Service, along with the OECD's Jacob Arturo Rivera Perez.

Ambassador Sybel Galván, from the Permanent Delegation of Mexico to the OECD, was instrumental in supporting the OECD in this project. The OECD Mexico Centre, under the leadership of Mario López, and the staff in charge of publications, notably Alejandro Camacho, also provided valuable support in co-ordinating the editorial process for the Spanish publication.

The report was reviewed by the OECD Working Party of Senior Public Integrity Officials (SPIO) on 13 April 2022 and approved by the Public Governance Committee on 13 May 2022. It was prepared for publication by the Secretariat.

Table of contents

FIGURES

TABLES

Follow OECD Publications on:

http://twitter.com/OECD_Pubs

http://www.facebook.com/OECDPublications

http://www.linkedin.com/groups/OECD-Publications-4645871

http://www.youtube.com/oecdilibrary

http://www.oecd.org/oecddirect/

Abbreviations and acronyms

AECF	Special Audit of Financial Compliance
	Auditoría Especial de Cumplimiento Financiero
AED	Special Audit of Performance
	Auditoría Especial de Desempeño
AEGF	Special Audit of Federal Spending
	Auditoría Especial de Gasto Federalizado
AESII	Special Audit of Monitoring, Reporting and Investigation
	Auditoría Especial de Seguimiento, Informes e Investigación
AIEG	Internal Audit and Management Evaluation Unit
	Auditoría Interna y de Evaluación de la Gestión
ASF	Superior Audit of the Federation
	Auditoría Superior de la Federación
DG	General Directorates
	Direcciones Generales
DGAF	General Directorate of Forensic Audits
	Dirección General de Auditoría Forense
DGATIC	General Directorate of Audit of Information and Communications Technology
	Dirección General de Auditoría de Tecnologías de Información y Comunicaciones
DGS	General Directorate of Systems
	Dirección General de Sistemas
EDN	National Digital Strategy
	Estrategia Digital Nacional
FGR	National Prosecutor's Office
	Fiscalía General de la República
NACS	National Anti-Corruption System
	Sistema Nacional Anticorrupción
NTS	National Transparency System
	Sistema Nacional de Transparencia
PND	National Development Plan
	Plan Nacional de Desarrollo
SAT	Tax Administration System

	Servicio de Administración Tributaria
SESNA	Executive Secretariat of the NACS
	Secretaría Ejecutiva del Sistema Nacional Anticorrupción
SFP	Ministry of Public Administration
	Secretaría de la Función Pública
SHCP	Ministry of Finance and Public Credit
	Secretaría de Hacienda y Crédito Público
SiCAF	System for the Control, Administration and Audit of Federal Expenditure Resources
	Sistema de Control, Administración y Fiscalización de los Recursos del Gasto Federalizado
SNF	National Auditing System
	Sistema Nacional de Fiscalización
TESOFE	Treasury of the Federation
	Tesorería de la Federación
UNEL	Unit of Regulation and Legislative Liasion
	Unidad de Normatividad y Enlace Legislativo

Executive summary

Main findings

The Supreme Audit Institution (SAI) of Mexico, the Superior Audit of the Federation (*Auditoría Superior de la Federación*, or ASF), recognises the critical role that data and analytics can play in the fulfilment of its mandate and achievement of strategic goals. Within the ASF, its digital transformation work programme emphasises ASF-wide goals and objectives for equipping auditors with the infrastructure, architecture, skills and tools needed to effectively audit in a digital environment. The COVID-19 pandemic has reinforced the need for this programme so that auditors have the necessary infrastructure and tools to audit remotely.

Data-driven risk detection and analytics for identifying corruption, fraud, waste and abuse (i.e. integrity risks), are critical elements of the ASF's strategy and activities for digital transformation. Taking advantage of data and analytics for identifying and assessing integrity risks does not typically occur in isolation from other data governance or analytics initiatives. For instance, improving data pre-processing for analysing fraud risks can have implications for data management policies and activities in other areas of the ASF's work, such as conducting performance audits. As a result, the report offers a range of proposals for the ASF to enhance its data governance and embed analytics into its strategic initiatives, drawing from good practices of other SAIs and accountability actors.

At the ASF, analytics and data governance are decentralised and split across multiple teams. For instance, the Special Audit of Financial Compliance (*Auditoría Especial de Cumplimiento Financiero*, AECF) and the Special Audit of Federal Spending (*Auditoría Especial del Gasto Federalizado, AEGF)* have developed their own unique initiatives, processes and capacities for analytics. This report also identifies operational priorities for the ASF to build its analytics capacity, particularly with regards to the integrity context, through improved co-ordination, digital skills development, and nurturing a data-centric culture. The review does not provide an exhaustive discussion of all of the ASF's applications of and capacity for leveraging analytics, or of the numerous ways auditors use data to support their work. The primary objective of the collaboration between the OECD and the ASF was to focus on data and analytics for integrity risk detection and the activities of the key teams working in this area, as identified by the ASF itself.

Recommendations

Chapter 1 emphasises that effective use of data and analytics requires taking an approach rooted in a strategy that all levels are aware of and can support. While the ASF has a digital strategy, which is best reflected in a digital transformation work programme, it does not articulate the use of data and analytics for preventing and detecting irregularities, a key area of the ASF's investment. Thus, efforts in this area are at risk of being uncoordinated and siloed. A clear strategy, with a unified vision for the organisation, can help the ASF articulate goals and objectives to avoid these pitfalls and instil a culture that promotes decision-driven analytics. In particular, a clearer vision for analytics as it relates to anti-corruption and integrity objectives could help engage leadership, enhance co-ordination, promote data-sharing internally, and facilitate the centralisation of key data activities in this area.

Chapter 1 also stresses the need for monitoring and continuous improvement in recognition of the evolving and dynamic nature of sustaining an analytics capacity. In taking a strategic approach, the ASF could ensure that plans for continuous improvement include periodic monitoring of new and existing initiatives, and assessing their return on investment. Having baselines and clearly defined objectives can improve decision making for new investments and the scaling-up of successful initiatives based on evidence and results.

Chapter 2 explores ways the ASF could benefit from greater co-ordination between the AECF and AEGF, which could include data-sharing pilots, institutionalising a cross-functional capacity, and carrying out an internal assessment to further explore and address capacity gaps. Data on their own do not have intrinsic value. Data become an asset only when applied effectively, and part of this means having the right people and well-co-ordinated institutional structures in place.

Chapter 2 also considers a number of tools and methodologies that are available to auditors to enhance the use of data and analytics for detecting integrity risks and irregularities, such as trend analysis, continuous monitoring through dashboards, and tools that can scrutinise both structured and unstructured data. The ASF could consider these tools, along with creating more robust feedback loops in order to more easily follow up on findings. In parallel, the chapter recommends that the ASF continue to promote a data-centric culture for sustaining future analytics initiatives. This entails building data literacy and a range of skills pertaining to analytics among staff, addressing themes related to privacy, safety, ethics and collaboration.

1 Strategic considerations for Mexico's supreme audit institution to advance analytics

Making effective use of data and analytics requires a strategy with clear goals and objectives that promote a coherent approach at all levels of the institution, as well as continuous learning to ensure impact. This chapter explores what it means for the ASF to take a "strategic approach" to data and analytics, focusing on assessing integrity risks. It covers both objective-setting at the institutional level, as well as the need for plans for the ASF to monitor its investment in analytics, drawing inspiration from other SAIs and OECD member countries.

1.1. Introduction

Making effective use of data and analytics requires more than simply introducing new tools, technologies or data sources to the work of audit institutions. It requires a strategy, with clear goals and objectives that all levels of the Supreme Audit Institution (SAI), particularly line managers and those charged with strategy implementation, are aware of and can support. A strategy helps the leadership of SAIs to be effective stewards of taxpayer money by ensuring that clear objectives guide investments and decisions. A strategy also provides incentives for continuous learning and aligning of data and analytics to long-term goals. Data and analytics serve institutional goals. Defining these goals and articulating them is a critical step in an organisation's digital transformation and instilling a culture that promotes decision-driven analytics as opposed to data-driven decision making (MIT, 2020[1]).

For Mexico's Superior Audit of the Federation (*Auditoria Superior de la Federación*, ASF), the digital strategy is best reflected in its digital transformation work programme, published in September 2020. The programme emphasises technical goals and objectives for equipping auditors with the infrastructure, architecture, skills and tools needed to effectively audit in a digital environment. By design, the programme focuses on many ASF-wide priorities, demonstrating the ASF's commitment internally and externally to invest in its own modernisation to keep pace with the digital transformation occurring across the Mexican government and among peer SAIs. Moreover, the COVID-19 pandemic further highlighted the importance of ASF's digital transformation, as reflected in different initiatives to enhance capacity for auditing remotely.

The digital transformation work programme sets the tone and a solid foundation for many activities. The document describing the programme notes that data can ultimately be used for real-time monitoring or for the use of artificial intelligence in auditing. However, it does not elaborate specifically on a key area of the ASF's investment—data and analytics for preventing and detecting irregularities.[1] As described in this report, the ASF has already developed several initiatives to collect data and assess integrity risks in support of its audits and investigations. However, without a clear institution-wide, unified strategy and objectives for leveraging data and analytics in this critical area of the ASF's activities, the institutional investments and efforts in terms of data and analytics are at risk of being siloed, ad hoc and inefficient. This chapter explores the need for the ASF to enhance its "strategic approach" to data and analytics for assessing integrity risks in terms of both objective-setting at the institutional level as well as putting in place the plans for the ASF to monitor its investment in analytics, drawing inspiration from other SAIs and OECD member countries.[2]

1.2. Setting the foundations for effective use of analytics for assessing integrity risks

The International Organization of Supreme Audit Institutions (INTOSAI) promotes the modernisation of SAIs through the issuing of standards and guidance that emphasise the critical role of data for supporting SAIs' missions. Specifically, INTOSAI calls on SAIs to take a strategic approach to how they use data. Several working groups and partners of INTOSAI, such as the Working Group on Information Technology Auditing and the INTOSAI Development Initiative, have issued practical guidance on how SAIs can accomplish this. Guidance for combating fraud and corruption also highlights the critical role that data and analytics can play, and the suggested policies, practices and tools for leveraging data in support of this specific objective. There is no single definition of "analytics" (used as shorthand for "data analytics" in this report). Analytics can be seen as the computation process of exploratory and confirmatory "data analysis", including data collection, cleansing, analysing and deploying (INTOSAI, 2019[2]). This report adopts this broad definition and conceptualisation of analytics given the relevance for the ASF and the focus of the project.

Box 1.1. Analytics guidelines of the INTOSAI Working Group on IT Audit

Analytics is a broad field, and even among supreme audit institutions, practices can vary widely depending on desired outcomes, available raw data, and context. However, the INTOSAI Working Group on IT Audit, of which the ASF is a member, has developed a series of general guidelines to bear in mind when using analytics to support audit work. These recommendations are subdivided into five chronological steps per INTOSAI (Figure 1.1).

- **Initial stage:** Identify the target or the objective, and a potential source of data to be used.
- **Data readiness:** Take a careful look at the potential data– cleanse it, and check for data reliability.
- **Analytics creation:** Decide how the data, once prepared, will be analysed. There are a number of different type of analytics methodologies, and it is critical the right one is selected for any specific project:
  - Descriptive analytics merely summarise the data available into simple percentages or fractions.
  - Diagnostic analytics are conducted to find out why something happened, or why something did not happen the way it should have.
  - Predictive analytics use data to estimate the likelihood of future events. Multiple linear regression or machine learning are well known examples. If a Machine Learning model is ultimately selected, an additional step known as training is also required at this stage. In training, the programme is taught what to look for and how to evaluate findings.
- **Analytics deployment:** Apply the analytics programme to the cleansed and ready data. This step could be a one-off, frequent, or continuous, depending on the programme selected.
- **Business intelligence:** Apply what was learned through the analytics programme to reporting and decision making.

Figure 1.1. INTOSAI's Data Analytics Process

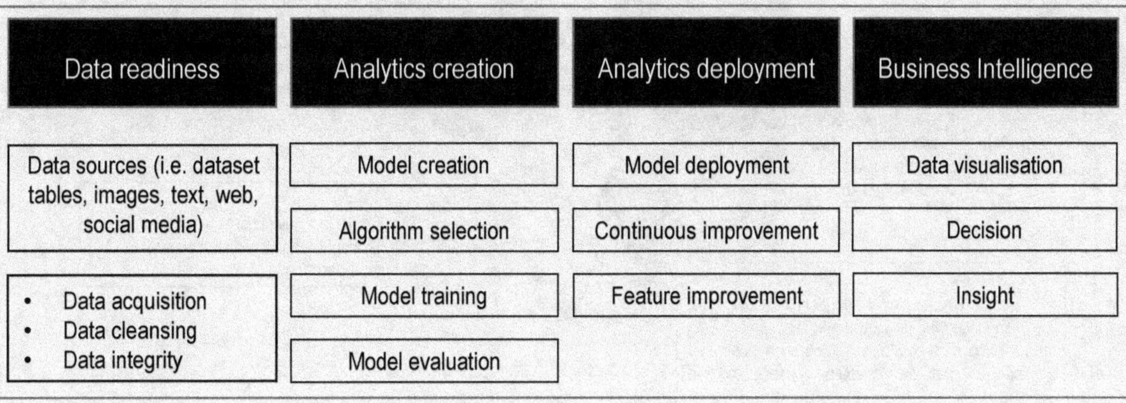

Source: (INTOSAI, 2019[2]).

The ASF's investment in its digital transformation aligns with broader trends in the Executive Branch of the federal government in recent years. In July 2019, the Federal Official Gazette (*Diario Oficial de la Federación*) published Mexico's 2019-2024 National Development Plan (*Plan Nacional de Desarrollo*, PND), which sets out the national objectives, strategy, and priorities for Mexico's development. From 2013 to 2018, the federal government pursued a National Digital Strategy (*Estrategia Digital Nacional*, EDN) that recognised the strategic value of digitalisation for the public sector and society in general (Government of Mexico, 2013[3]). The government did not implement a new strategy after 2018, although the National Digital Strategy Office (*Coordinación de la Estrategia Digital Nacional*, CEDN) at the Office of the President in Mexico is considering a new one (Coordination of the National Digital Strategy, Government of Mexico, 2021[4]). The "National Programme to Combat Corruption and Impunity, and to Improve Public Management" for 2019-2024—led by SFP, CEDN and the Ministry of Finance and Public Credit (*Secretaría de Hacienda y Crédito Público*, SHCP)—provides strategic direction and priorities that focus specifically on anti-corruption.

While Mexico lacks an updated National Digital Strategy, the National Development Plan and anti-corruption programmes provide direction for the strategic use of data. Data governance is at the core of many of the principles and policies that the Mexican government has adopted in recent years. Robust data governance promotes integration and systemic coherence, offering a common basis for organisations to effectively use data for a range of policy goals, including combatting corruption and fraud. The model described in Figure 1.2 highlights the values of all organisational, policy and technical aspects for successful data governance.

Figure 1.2. Aspects for successful data governance

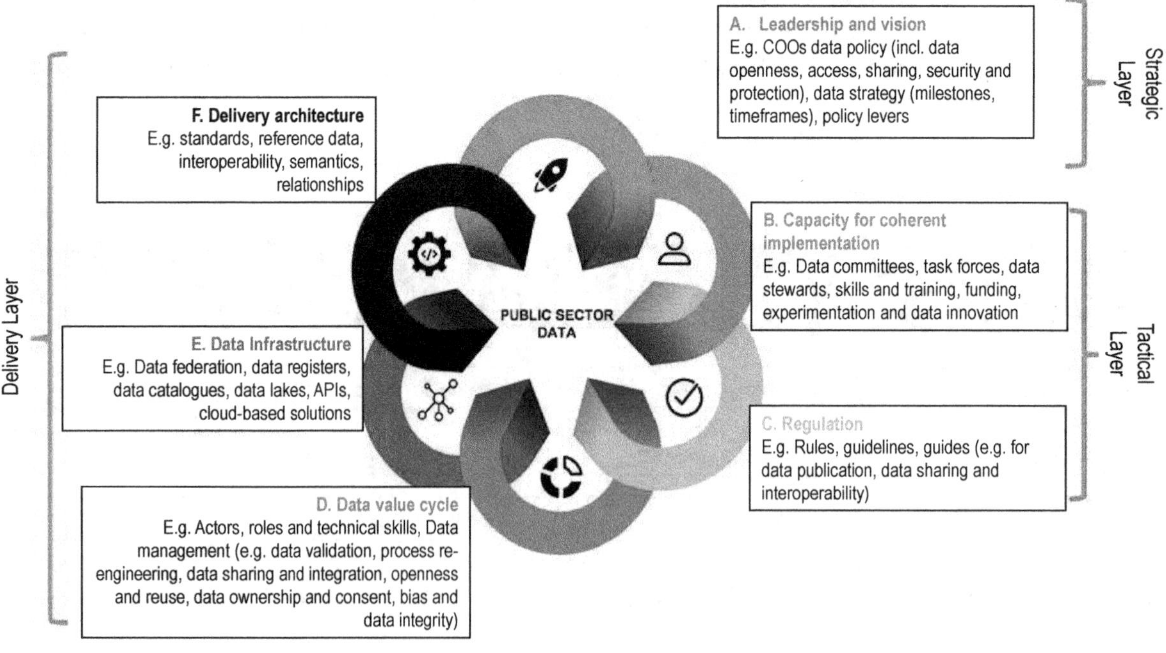

Source: (OECD, 2019[5]).

The data governance model above is relevant from both a whole-of-government and institutional perspective. For audit institutions, data governance and data management are at the forefront of their everyday work. INTOSAI's Moscow Declaration calls for SAIs to make better use of data and analytics in audits, including "adaptation strategies, such as planning for such audits, developing experienced teams for data analytics, and introducing new techniques into the practice of public audit" (INTOSAI, 2019[6]). Moreover, various INTOSAI regional and working groups, as well as individual SAIs, have raised the need for effective data governance as the "what" and "how" of auditing evolves with the digitalisation of government.[3] Government entities beyond SAIs are grappling with the same issues and developing their own data governance framework (see the example from New Zealand in Box 1.2). The model in Figure 1.3 captures common principles and needs across these sources, including:

- **The strategic layer** demonstrated that data strategies are a critical element of good data governance. Data strategies enable accountability and can help define leadership, expectations, roles and goals. The strategic layer also highlights how the formulation of data policies and/or strategies can benefit from open and participatory processes, thus integrating the inputs of actors from within ASF and externally.

- **The tactical layer** enables the coherent implementation and steering of data policies, strategies and initiatives. It draws upon the value of auditors' skills and competencies, and highlights people-centred activities like recruitment, communication, co-ordination, and collaboration as instruments for extracting value from data assets. It also takes into account the importance of formal and informal institutional networks, such as communities of practice. The tactical layer also includes data-related legislation and regulations that help to define and ensure compliance with the rules and policies guiding data management, including data openness, protection and sharing.

- **The delivery layer** covers the day-to-day implementation of data strategies. It touches on different technical and policy aspects of the data value cycle across its different stages (from data production to reuse), the role and interaction of different actors in each stage (e.g. as data providers), and the inter-connection of data flows across stages. The adoption of technological solutions takes place in this layer with a linkage to strategic goals and objectives. It also relates, for instance, to the need for re-engineering legacy infrastructure, architecture and data management practices and processes. Addressing issues of data interoperability and standardisation also takes place at this level.

In interviews, ASF officials highlighted aspects of all six key elements—leadership and vision; capacity; regulation; data value cycle; data infrastructure; and data architecture—as challenges. In particular, several strategic priorities including establishing a unified vision for analytics for integrity, collaborating more closely with other institutions, and devising a cohesive action plan came to the forefront during fact-finding interviews with the OECD, as discussed below. These priorities are critical because they are the foundation for effective and efficient use of analytics that avoids creating data siloes and promotes efficiency across ASF on cross-cutting activities that are resource intensive, such as data management and cleaning. The subsequent sections take inspiration from these elements as a framework for identifying areas for ASF to improve its own approach to data and analytics for detecting integrity risks.

Box 1.2. Data Governance Framework of New Zealand

The leading agency for government-held data in New Zealand (Stats NZ) developed a new and improved data governance framework for the New Zealand government. The framework is part of the agency's numerous efforts to promote better data management practices across the public sector, and to leverage data as a strategic asset for decision making. One of the central pillars of the framework is the adoption of a so-called "whole-of-data life cycle approach", meaning public bodies and employees are encouraged to think more strategically about the governance, management, quality and accountability of their data, over the whole data life cycle (i.e. from the design and source of the data to its storing, publication and disposal).

Figure 1.3. Towards a holistic data governance framework

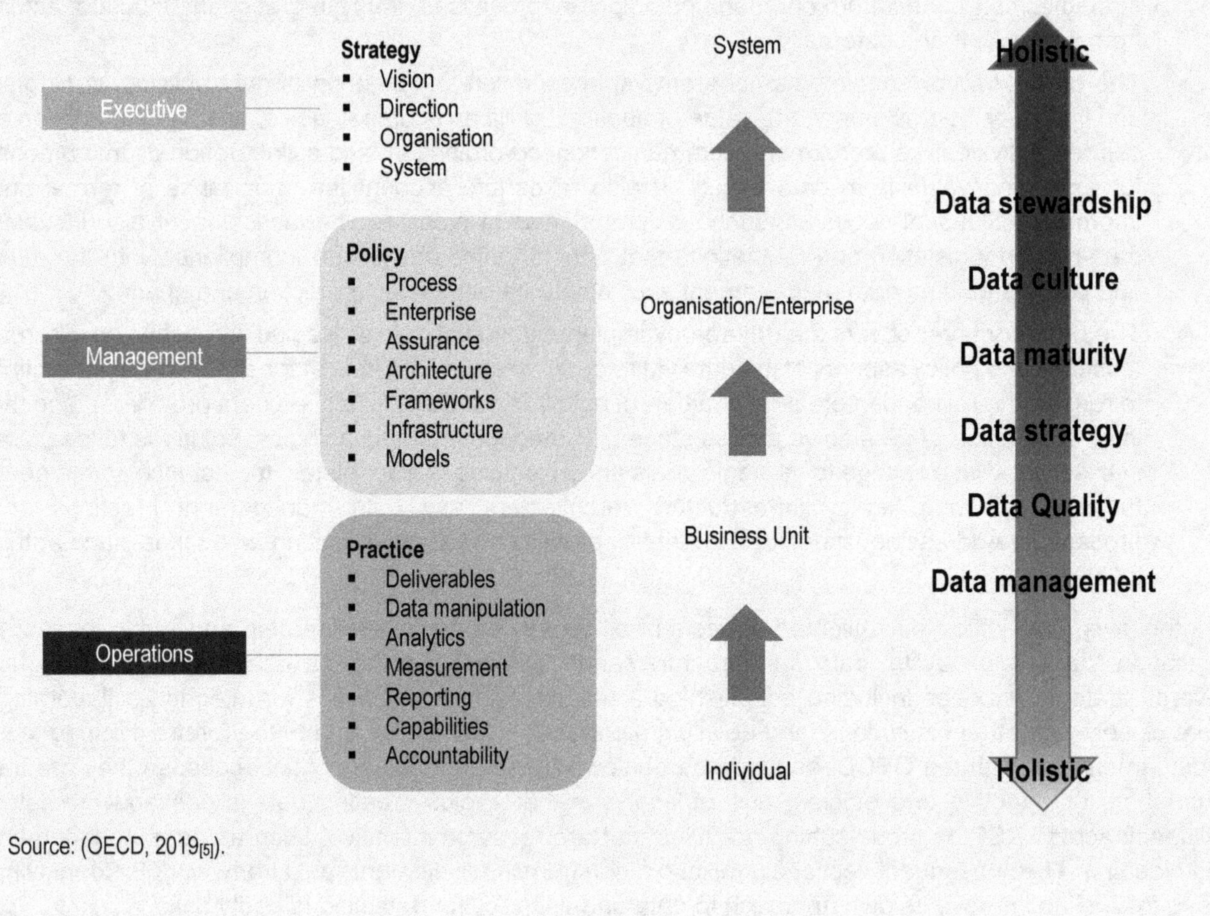

Source: (OECD, 2019[5]).

1.3. Approaching analytics with a strategic mindset

1.3.1. Establishing a unified vision for analytics

While the National Development Plan provides broader goals for government to navigate digital transformation, and ASF's role in the NACS provides some inspiration, ASF can set objectives for digital transformation and analytics at its discretion. ASF's strategic plan for 2018-2026 consists of 29 objectives that map across a theory of change for contributing to good governance and accountability in the public sector, as well as positioning ASF as a national and international example of high quality technical expertise. One of the main value propositions of ASF described in its strategic plan is to raise awareness among audited entities about the risks of irregularities. The plan also emphasises the need for risk analyses, "leading" technologies to support ASF's functions, and the development of technical capabilities and the specialisation of staff (ASF, 2018[7]). However, the strategy does not articulate clear goals or objectives that set a unified vision or guide for teams within the ASF that have developed independent initiatives for using data and analytics to assess integrity risks.

Likewise, the ASF's digital work programme does not provide a unified vision, objectives or direction. In addition to the strategic plan, ASF's General Directorate of Systems (*Dirección General de Sistemas,* DGS) developed a work programme to guide the digital transformation. The DGS sits within the General Administration Unit (*Unidad General de Administración*), and among other roles, has a strategic cross-cutting function to establish IT standards, policies and systems within the ASF, as well as implement technical tools and provide technical assistance internally (Government of Mexico, 2021[8]). The digital transformation programme elaborates a multi-dimensional objective to:

> *Develop, regulate and implement projects of substantive and procedural processes with automated flows that consider inputs and outputs in digital format, from robotic automation, electronic signature and signature of the Tax Administration System (SAT) and time stamps of the Ministry of Economy (SE), to the storage of information and critical transactions in blockchain in order to promote the digital transformation in the Superior Audit of the Federation that ensures the availability of "state-of-the-art" technologies to strengthen the institution, stay at the forefront in use of existing technology and enhance the results of the audit of public resources (ASF, 2020[9]).*

The programme also highlights several projects that are relevant for analytics, including the development of a central data warehouse, automation of data processes and information flow, and the digitalisation of the ASF's audit process through the development of a Digital Mailbox (*Buzón Digital*) (ASF, 2020[9]).

The ASF's strategy and digital work programme broadly allude to analytics and integrity risks, but they do not outline objectives that link analytics for identifying irregularities. Data and analytics enable teams across the ASF to achieve their objectives, and deliver on the institution's broader value propositions as defined in its strategic plan. In interviews with senior ASF officials, establishing a unified vision for data and analytics, including one that reflects auditing and governance trends related to big data, was flagged as one of the ASF's top strategic priorities. Addressing analytics at the strategic level could have a number of positive impacts on ASF's digital transformation. For instance, in interviews, officials recognised that it would be useful to engage leadership, enhance co-ordination, promote data sharing internally and potentially facilitate the centralisation of key data activities (see section below). It could also help leadership to establish experimentation as a strategic objective, and frame efforts to innovate as part of the ASF's culture and management's commitment to invest in auditors' skills and tools (see Chapter 2). Box 1.3 illustrates how the Australian National Audit Office (ANAO) addresses data and analytics in its corporate plan, which is the ANAO's core document for setting its vision and strategic directions.

Box 1.3. The Australian National Audit Office's strategic priorities for data and analytics

Taking a unified, cohesive, and strategic approach on data analytics is critically important for audit institutions hoping to maximise resources, improve decision making and achieve the organisation's goals. With this in mind, the Australian National Audit Office (ANAO)'s yearly corporate plan sets out a clear and succinct framework for how data analytics and technology will be used at the organisation, the specific and relevant processes in place, and which teams across the organisation are responsible for each aspect. More specifically, the document identifies a stand-alone team dedicated to analytics, key areas in which the Office would like to use data to better meet its objectives, and ways in which it would like to improve data governance practices. The importance of data analytics to the organisation's work is also highlighted by its mention in other related sections of the corporate plan, including those on human capital, budgeting and productivity.

Source: (Australian National Audit Office, 2020[10]).

1.3.2. Creating an action plan for analytics

The ASF's approach to analytics can be characterised as bottom-up, with specialised areas developing capacities, tools and processes that serve their individual mandates, which include assessing integrity risks. Nonetheless, as noted above, the ASF does not have clearly defined objectives or processes for identifying integrity risks through analytics, and those that are in place are not unified across teams. Its expertise in data and analytics for this purpose is spread across four different departments—"Superior Audits"—and their General Directorates (*Direcciones Generales*, DG). This includes the Special Audit of Financial Compliance (*Auditoría Especial de Cumplimiento Financiero*, AECF) and within it, the General Directorate of Forensic Audits (*Dirección General de Auditoría Forense*, DGAF) and the General Directorate of Audit of Information and Communications Technology (*Dirección General de Auditoría de Tecnologías de Información y Comunicaciones*, DGATIC). These DGs have concentrated resources of data and analytics experts.

In addition, expertise in analytics can be found in other departments that have developed their own capacities independently, including the Special Audit of Federal Spending (*Auditoría Especial de Gasto Federalizado,* AEGF*)*, as well as the Special Audit of Performance (*Auditoría Especial de Desempeño*, AED). In late August 2021, ASF issued amended internal regulations that introduced a DG under the auspices of the AEGF, called the DG of Forensic Audit and Federal Spending (*Dirección General de Auditoría Forense del Gasto Federalizado, DGAFGF*).[4] The fourth department-level team in the ASF, the Special Audit of Monitoring, Reporting and Investigation (*Auditoría Especial de Seguimiento, Informes e Investigación*, AESII) plays a more indirect role, as it supports the follow-up of audits and referrals that use the analytics produced by other departments.

Both the AECF and the AEGF have also developed independent systems and approaches to analytics to support auditors within their respective departments, detailed further in Chapter 2. These systems leverage different databases, but they share many of the same processes and challenges concerning data management, and even share some of the same data sources. The AECF has also developed innovative applications of new technologies to support the ASF's auditing across the institution. This includes the use of satellite imagery to enhance remote oversight, such as audits of infrastructure projects. It also involves the use of geographic information systems and geo-referencing tools to inform analysis of territorial gaps in auditing and organise the results of audits over the last 20 years to allow for filtering by geography. The AECF envisioned the enhancement of new tools in 2021, such as the use of drones to facilitate real-time auditing of public works and the development of dashboards with key performance indicators. The AECF's work not only has wide implications for other departments in the ASF, but it is also addressing needs related to improving the use of data and analytics for detecting fraud, as discussed in Chapter 2.

As the name suggests, the mission of the DGAF is to conduct forensic audits and investigations, and according to the DGAF officials, the DG makes use of data and forensic tools for all of the audits it conducts. The DGAF also hosts the ASF's Forensic Laboratory (*Laboratorio Forense*), which collects, analyses and safeguards the digital evidence in adherence with regulations and chain of custody procedures (ASF, 2021[11]). The Forensic Laboratory is not a centralised data and analytics function, although some activities include data analysis and it does support other DGs primarily within the AECF. The main objectives of the Forensic Laboratory are to 1) obtain and safeguard digital evidence; 2) analyse physical storage devices or digital information that may be considered as evidence or support for any alleged irregularity and subsequent sanction procedures; and 3) provide analysis and support for investigations. Its activities include:

- Creation of forensic images of electronic devices in order to preserve and ensure the integrity of the information.
- Recovery and analysis of digital information focused on the review of different digital data sources through the application of specific software.
- Data analyses, including data matching and other techniques.
- Network analysis and visualisations to support investigations.
- Assessment of counterfeit documentation and fraudulent imitation of text in electronic files.
- Data management and copying information between physical storage devices, and if necessary, identifying possible errors linked to corrupt data or anomalies.
- Secure deletion of physical storage devices (ASF, 2021[11]).

To complement the strategic plan and work programme on digital transformation, the ASF could devise an action plan that focuses on institutional objectives for leveraging data and analytics to enhance audit work. The ASF's own work programme for digital transformation covers several critical areas that could be reflected in the action plan. For instance, the work programme includes analyses of the ASF's strengths, weaknesses, opportunities and threats (SWOT) across key components of the entity's digital transformation objectives. This includes analyses of the ASF's objectives related to software development, technological infrastructure, telecommunications, computer services and systems operations. All of these areas influence the ability of auditors to make use of data in their work. What differentiates an action plan from this work programme is the ability to hone in on applications of data and analytics in specific areas of ASF's activities, which in turn helps to tailor digital transformation to the goals and needs of different teams. One of these areas could be data and analytics for assessing integrity risks, filling a critical gap in the attention the ASF currently pays to fraud and corruption in its strategy and digital transformation work programme.

The European Court of Auditors (ECA) is undergoing its own digital transformation. This includes efforts to exercise greater automation in its audit procedures, employ algorithms to detect irregularities in digital documents and make use of artificial intelligence to detect performance patterns in large datasets (The European Court of Auditors, 2019[12]). According to the ECA, such innovations can make it so auditors focus more on asking the right questions rather than spending all their time on verification and analyses. As ASF advances its own digital transformation, an action plan will help the ASF to go beyond its current approach to identify objectives that are specific, measurable, achievable, relevant and time-based relative to specific areas. The ECA's road map, with a focus on short, medium and long-term objectives, may serve as a model for the ASF to set priorities and frame its own path forward in the action plan. Implicit in this figure is the notion that the ASF could consider a phased approach to its enhancement of analytics over the period of several years. This is similar to what the UK National Audit Office (NAO) has done to deliver its own strategic transformation. In the first year, the NAO completed a detailed plan and started to procure new audit software and rolled out a cloud-based data platform (i.e. the Audit Information Management System), while developing a data-driven methodology to assess risks related to audited entities. In 2021-22, the NAO will pilot the methodology and will implement it fully the following year (UK National Audit Office, 2021[13]).

Figure 1.4. The European Court of Auditor's roadmap towards digital audit

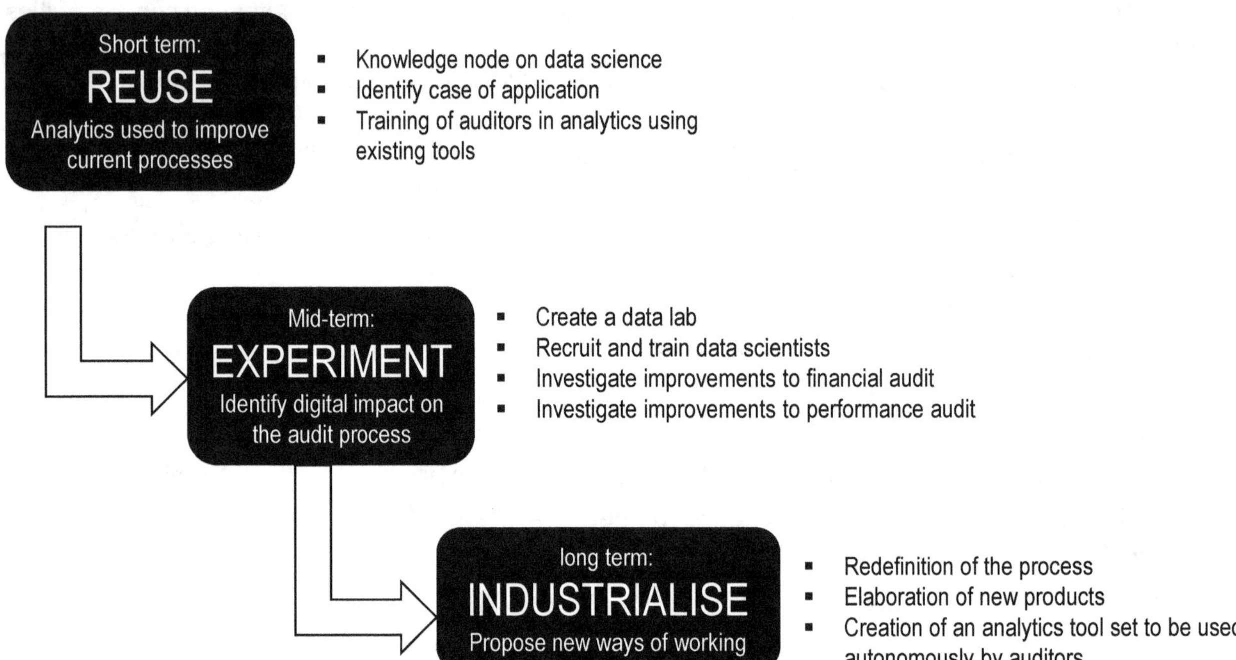

Source: (The European Court of Auditors, 2019[12]).

The value of developing an action plan lies in large part in the process itself. Given their mandates, the Directorate General of Planning and Evaluation (*Dirección General de Planeación y Evaluación*) or the DGS, would likely take leadership roles in this effort. What is critical, regardless of which Directorate steers the action plan, is that the DGs have direct reporting lines to senior leadership and an institution-wide mandate. For instance, when the UK National Audit Office enhanced its analytics and established an internal data service, one of the key enablers of its efforts was the leveraging of senior leadership (UK National Audit Office, 2018[14]). However, development of the action plan would be a vehicle for engaging and gaining support from a wider range of actors, including the departments and teams that are responsible for data management and analytics across the ASF, as described below. A collective effort to develop an analytics action plan would help to break down siloes between the different departments and teams that are working with similar data and using comparable techniques, as well as facing similar challenges related to capacity and data access (see more on co-ordination in Chapter 2). The action plan would also help to encourage staff to consider how data can support the planning and execution of audits, and create an organisational culture around the subject. In addition to engaging leadership early and often, other considerations for the ASF in terms of the development process and content of an action plan, some of which are elaborated on in Chapter 2, include:

- Using the data governance framework described above to help frame key areas to focus on and identify priorities.
- Considering implications and relevance for the entire audit cycle, including planning, implementation and follow-up.

- Defining clear objectives as part of the action plan so that purpose comes before the data, and not the other way around.
- Accounting for internal context by making objective and activities tailored and fit-for-purpose for individual team's within the ASF.
- Promoting learning, inclusivity and experimentation when using data and new techniques.
- Establishing indicators and a theory of change for the ASF with regards to data and analytics, focusing on outcomes and not simply outputs (e.g. indicators that reflect fraud loss prevention, mitigation or recoveries as a result of data and analytics).
- Developing a baseline for measuring the impact of the ASF's investments in analytics, and a starting point for making changes in response to internal and external factors, such as changes in funding or the need to respond to emerging risks in the context of COVID-19.
- Accounting for the external context and stakeholders (e.g. the ASF's own digital transformation work programme describes key external stakeholders that would be relevant and the COVID-19 crisis can help to shape priorities).

Brazil's supreme audit institution (*Tribunal de Contas da União*, TCU), developed its own analytics capacity in a similar way, albeit with a more deliberate strategic decision to decentralise its analytics capacities to audit teams. Individual departments trained auditors in analytics, encouraged them to seek data and technological support tools that would be useful for their audits, and form communities of practice. To illustrate for the ASF how the TCU approached a similar task, Box 1.4 describes the three key pillars it chose to structure its data analysis strategy—governance, a platform and information-based solutions.

Box 1.4. Pillars of data and analytics strategy of Brazil's supreme audit institution

Organisations strive to work effectively and efficiently, which can sometimes be alternatively articulated as *doing better, but also choosing what is done better*. This same idea can be applied to audit institutions, which, given their constrained resources, frequently face steep opportunity costs on project selection decisions. Analytics can make these decisions easier, but often the increasingly vast amount of information and seemingly infinite possibilities for analysis can hamper efforts towards efficiency and effectiveness. Thus, institutions must formalise and implement work processes to ensure that analytics are indeed improving the body's work – that the information being used is necessary and sufficient to fill its purpose. Brazil's Supreme Audit institution, the *Tribunal de Contas da União* (TCU), did this by focusing on the three following main pillars.

- **Governance:** the guidelines, support and direction that come from top management, including a cohesive organisational strategy and a plan of action. This can help create a culture within the organisation that encourages the use of analytics for control activities.
- **Platform:** the tangible tools needed to execute analytics-related tasks – to derive useful insights from raw data. For example, TCU created and manages a virtual environment named *Labcontas*. *Labcontas* allows auditors to easily and independently access information from dozens of databases as a benefit of agreements signed between public institutions. This makes it easier to co-ordinate efforts, and reduces the time and resources often needed to obtain information during audits.
- **Information-based solutions:** the tools and the high-level structures put in place must result in actionable, timely and reliable insights. This kind of information is used in Brazil for a range of audit-related tasks, from holding managers accountable to flagging potential high-risk grant or procurement proposals submitted to the government.

Source: (Revista do TCU, 2016[15]).

1.3.3. Engaging the National Digital Platform and the Ministry of Public Administration

In July 2016, the Mexican government signed into law the National Anti-Corruption System (*Sistema Nacional Anticorrupción*, NACS). The NACS forms part of a series of broader reforms for improved governance in Mexico, and is closely linked with complementary initiatives that established the National Auditing and National Transparency System (NAS and NTS, respectively). Together, these "systems" of accountability and integrity actors were conceived in order to strengthen anti-corruption, oversight and transparency measures in the Mexican government. The General Law of the NACS (*Ley General del Sistema Nacional Anticorrupción*) provides that a representative of a Citizen Participation Committee (CPC) presides over the system's Co-ordination Committee and Governing Board, composed of the heads of the Ministry of Public Administration (*Secretaría de Función Pública*, SFP); the ASF; the Federal Tribunal of Administrative Justice (*Tribunal Federal de Justicia Administrativa*); the Specialised Anticorruption Prosecutor (*Fiscalía Especializada en Combate a la Corrupción*); the National Institute for Transparency, Access to Information and the Protection of Personal Data (*Instituto Nacional de Transparencia, Acceso a la Información y Protección de Datos Personales*); and a representative from the Federal Judicial Council (*Consejo de la Judicatura Federal*) (Government of Mexico, 2021[16]).

The General Law also established the National Digital Platform (*Plataforma Digital Nacional*, PDN). The goal of the platform is to support the work of the authorities of the NACS with new technologies, methodologies, data science and artificial intelligence (National Anti-Corruption System, 2021[17]). The PDN also aims to reduce siloes of information so that data can be comparable, accessible, and reusable (Executive Secretary of the National Anti-Corruption System, Mexico, 2020[18]). The PDN aims to provide access to the following systems and sources of information:

- asset and proof of presentation of tax declarations
- public servants involved in public procurement procedures
- sanctioned public servants and private individuals
- information and communication of the NACS and NAS
- complaints for administrative offenses and acts of corruption
- public information on procurement.

In 2019, the OECD issued a follow-up report of a 2017 *Integrity Review of Mexico* that provided recommendations in a number of areas, including proposals for addressing the challenges in the design of the PDN (OECD, 2019[19]). The recommendations focused on ensuring the interoperability of databases and developing a strategy for using the platform effectively for risk analysis. By September 2019, the Executive Secretariat of the NACS (*Secretaría Ejecutiva del Sistema Nacional Anticorrupción*, SESNA) had launched the beta version of the PDN. At the time of drafting this report, the PDN is still in its first version, and the SESNA had successfully incorporated four of the six databases (National Anti-Corruption System, 2021[17]). The SESNA has yet to incorporate data on complaints and data related to information and communication of the NACS and the NAS into the PDN. This reflects what the SESNA describes as a significant ongoing challenge of accessing and collecting data from across government (Executive Secretary of the National Anti-Corruption System, Mexico, 2020[18]).

As a leader of both the NACS and NAS, the ASF is well-positioned to accelerate the improvements to the PDN described in the OECD's 2017 report, including addressing gaps in data, enhancing the quality of data and helping to fulfil the promise of the PDN as an effective tool for risk analysis. Regarding data quality, ASF officials noted that auditors can use the PDN, but they still must substantiate their findings with certified information obtained directly from the relevant authority. The ASF could promote and support improvements to the quality of data on the PDN based on the experience of ASF's auditors and their follow-up to certify data. In turn, this could help to improve the quality of the ASF's (and others') analyses based on the PDN.

Moreover, a deeper engagement to accelerate improvements to the PDN would also be a constructive avenue for the ASF to further engage with the NACS and the NAS, in accordance with its mandate under the General Law of the National Anticorruption System, while supporting the implementation of Mexico's anti-corruption agenda.[5] Recent media accounts have criticised the NACS for not fulfilling its mandate and in a recent study, Mexico scored poorly on implementation of anti-corruption laws. For instance, a 2020 study showed that while Mexico has a strong anti-corruption legal framework, it stands out relative to eight other countries in Latin America for its lack of implementation of laws and reduced institutional capacity (Lawyers Council for Civil and Economic Rights, 2020[20]). Initiatives related to data and analytics could help to address implementation challenges and generate positive attention for the NACS and the ASF among the general public. For instance, the ASF, the SFP and other members of the NACS and the NAS could also consider developing guidance for government to enhance data quality for the PDN, drawing inspiration from the United Kingdom's National Fraud Initiative (NFI). The NFI's platform operates differently from the PDN, since public bodies are required to submit data to the NFI on a regular basis. However, the underlying data issues the NFI faces are similar to the Mexican context. The NFI produces guidance that sets out data specifications in terms of how data should be formatted and the types of data checks entities can conduct. It also supports the ethical use of data through initiatives like the *Code of Data Matching Practice*, which promotes transparency and lays out principles and practices for protecting citizens' right to privacy (see Box 1.5).

Box 1.5. The UK National Fraud Initiative's Code of Data Matching Practice

The Audit Commission's National Fraud Initiative was launched in 1996 as the United Kingdom's largest data-matching exercise in relation to fraud. The Serious Crime Act of 2007 enabled bodies, other than those with a mandatory requirement to provide data for the National Fraud Initiative, to volunteer to participate by providing data to the commission (Government of the UK, 2007[21]).

The National Fraud Initiative has enabled participating organisations to prevent and detect more than GBP 300 million fraud and error in the period from April 2016 to March 2018. Approximately 1 200 public and private sector organisations participate in the initiative, including the public audit agencies in Scotland, Wales and Northern Ireland. Each national audit agency carries out data-matching under its own powers, but uses the National Fraud Initiative's systems, processes and expertise.

To increase transparency around this massive data-matching exercise, the National Fraud Initiative has set out a *Code of Data Matching Practice* that is followed by all organisations that participate in the Cabinet Office's data-matching exercises. The code "creates a balance between the important public policy objective of preventing and detecting fraud, and the need to pay due regard to the rights of those whose data are matched for this purpose." To achieve this goal, the code was informed by the consultation of a range of stakeholders, with the Information Commissioner's office providing input on data protection.

The code notably requires each institution to publish a privacy notice that informs citizens about the specific datasets used, the way they are collected, the purpose of this data-matching exercise and its legal basis, the institutions with which the data are shared, the retention period for the data, and the rights of citizens including complaint mechanisms.

This example illustrates both the necessity of transparency for integrity actors when implementing anti-fraud programmes and the value of their input to inform the creation of codes of practice that safeguard citizen's rights.

Source: (Cabinet Office's National Fraud Initiative, Government of the UK, 2018[22]).

The ASF could also consider enhancing its co-ordination with SFP concerning data use and reuse, and detecting integrity risks. The ASF focuses on *ex post* auditing whereas the SFP, as the internal audit function, provides monitoring and assurance throughout the year, so it is unlikely there is duplication, according to ASF officials. Officials also noted that they inform the SFP and the audited entity if they detect irregularities during an audit. However, as noted in the next chapter, communication between the ASF and the SFP as an objective of co-ordination is a low intensity effort. Building on this, the ASF and the SFP could work together to identify shared objectives and additional avenues for collaboration. For instance, in the context of analytics for assessing integrity risks, the ASF and the SFP could exchange risk registries and convene regular meetings to better co-ordinate responses and outreach to the Specialised Anticorruption Prosecutor, a unit within the National Prosecutor's Office (*Fiscalía General de la República*, FGR), when irregularities are found. This process is currently lacking a co-ordinated approach, ASF officials recognised.[6] There are already precedents. According to officials, ASF has entered into agreements for the exchange of information with several institutions, including the Tax Administration Service (SAT), the SHCP and the Treasury of the Federation (TESOFE), among others.[7]

1.4. Planning and monitoring for continuous improvement

1.4.1. Developing a plan to monitor existing and new analytics initiatives

The ASF could develop a plan to ensure the relevance of its analytics initiatives and reliability of the results, particularly for new methodologies and systems that are under development. The ASF can lead by example and draw from its own standards for internal control (*Marco Integrado de Control Interno*). According to the standards, managers of government entities should use monitoring and evaluation to identify problems in a timely manner and implement corrective actions (ASF, 2014[23]). The ASF is primarily a consumer of data, and the models and systems it develops for running analytics are subject to changes over time. This can include changes to data quality or relevance, depending on the methodology. For instance, ASF officials highlighted plans within the AECF to develop a machine learning capacity. Machine learning relies on the use of historical data to develop algorithms and predictive models. Shifts in context, data reliability or data access can affect the accuracy and utility of the model. For this reason, continuous monitoring of the performance of the ASF's data and analytics initiatives is a critical component of the aforementioned action plan, should ASF decide to develop one.

Monitoring makes up one of four key pillars in the GAO's Artificial Intelligence (AI) Accountability Framework, which also includes governance, data and performance. GAO developed the AI Framework to support managers in using AI responsibly and to promote accountability in government AI programmes and processes. GAO identified key practices that focus on the design, development, deployment, and continuous monitoring of AI systems, organised into the four pillars. Many of the activities across each of the pillars support or serve a monitoring or evaluative purpose, which can offer the ASF insights into what it can monitor for its own analytics initiatives. For instance, the "Data" pillar highlights the need for government entities to document sources and origins used for data models, including documents on 1) the means of collecting, preparing, labelling and maintaining data; and 2) the means of monitoring data on a continual basis (US Government Accountability Office, 2021[24]). Box 1.6 provides further details on the AI Framework's monitoring pillar.

> ## Box 1.6. The monitoring pillar of the US Government Accountability Office's Artificial Intelligence Accountability Framework
>
> Like other government entities, audit bodies that use AI must continuously monitor these programmes to ensure that they are still conducting analysis the way they were intended to. The US Government Accountability Office (GAO) includes two components of this type of AI monitoring, continuous monitoring and assessing sustainment for expanded use of AI. As part of its AI framework, the GAO describes leading practices for each of these components.
>
> ### Continuous monitoring of performance
>
> When monitoring for performance, government entities should consider implementing plans that outline when and how the AI will be checked. In general, AI that has a high impact on an entity's work should be subject to increased monitoring. Another possible step to produce accurate results would be to establish the range of data and model drift that is acceptable to ensure the AI system produces desired results. Input data and output from the AI also requires verification when monitoring AI. The GAO stipulates that entities should document findings and results from monitoring to promote transparency and accountability. Monitoring should also involve conducting interviews and consultations with key stakeholders.
>
> ### Assessing for sustainment and expanded use
>
> To assess sustainment, audit bodies should assess whether the AI programme is still relevant to the present context, and if it is still meeting organisational requirements. Novel areas in which use of the AI may be expanded should also be considered. This could involve conducting third party assessments.
>
> Source: (US Government Accountability Office, 2021[24]).

Monitoring for continuous improvement can also help the ASF to identify the extent of false positives, and understand how to refine its analytics to ensure resources and control activities are targeted appropriately. No analytics technique is fail proof, and human error can be difficult to decipher from fraud or corruption based on what essentially amounts to a review of databases. Human biases can also seep into algorithms and analyses (see Box 1.7). The ASF's auditors follow-up on irregularities (see next chapter), but capacity is limited and feedback loops so that auditors learn about the results of their work from stakeholders (e.g. SFP, prosecutors offices or law enforcement) are ad hoc. The monitoring plan for data and analytics can help to address this issue by promoting communication and engagement of stakeholders, which in turn can help the ASF to refine its algorithms and analytics based on actual results.

Box 1.7. Monitoring biases in algorithms

Independence is an important component of the work of any auditor, and this fundamental principle can be extended to AI programmes used in audits as well. Biased AI models can be created by purposeful or accidental action, and can disproportionately harm groups or individuals, leading to concerning lapses of fairness and equity. For example, an AI software developed by a major technology company to pre-screen job applicants was found to be biased against female candidates. Damages to fairness and equity caused by an AI can diminish trust in governments, and therefore, AI programmes must be monitored regularly. Monitoring AI presents a number of challenges. It is possible that local laws prohibit the collection or use of certain forms of demographic data, and even if biases are found, it can be difficult to find the right approach to mitigating them. However, as a countermeasure to these challenges, governments are increasingly taking steps to offer guidance on monitoring AI for biases, and auditing AI models.

For instance, in the United Kingdom, the Centre for Data Ethics and Innovation (CDEI) is a government entity under the Department for Digital, Culture, Media and Sport that is tasked with developing the right governance regime for data-driven technologies. Specifically, the CDEI offers guidance on effective use of AI in government. It recommends that organisations using AI should frequently compare the data that was used to train an AI model against the population from which it was taken to ensure the former is representative. Secondly, managers of AI programmes should analyse and mitigate any other sources of bias that are likely to lead to differences in outcome. Finally, it is important to understand and analyse the correlation between key model variables and demographic groups to understand how these might impact biases and outcomes.

Source: (Centre for Data Ethics and Innovation, 2020[25]).

1.4.2. Assess the return on investment of analytics initiatives

According to the INTOSAI Framework of Professional Pronouncements (INTOSAI-P 12 on the Value and Benefits of Supreme Audit Institutions), the extent to which SAIs can make a difference in the lives of citizens depends on 12 principles.[8] One of these principles is that SAIs should be responsive to changing environments and emerging risks in order to demonstrate ongoing relevance to citizens, parliament and other stakeholders (INTOSAI, 2019[26]). To fulfil this principle, in part, SAIs should establish mechanisms for gathering information, making decisions and measuring performance. How SAIs do this varies, but the SAI Performance Measurement Framework, which the ASF helped to develop when it chaired the INTOSAI Working Group on the Value and Benefits of SAIs, provides general guidance for SAIs to assess results across a range of activities (INTOSAI, 2016[27]).

As described in the OECD's *Progress Report on the Implementation of the Mexican Superior Audit of the Federation's Mandate*, the ASF has a dedicated team in the Technical Unit called the Directorate of Analysis and Follow-up of Management (*Dirección de Análisis y Seguimiento de la Gestión*), which assesses the impact of ASF's work (OECD, 2021[28]). A key metric the team developed frames the ASF's impact as a function of recoveries relative to its overall budget (i.e. amount of recoveries from the audited public account divided by the modified budget assigned to the ASF for the fiscal year equals pesos recovered for each peso of modified budget). The sources of information for calculating this return on investment (ROI) are the annual General Executive Report that is delivered to the Surveillance Commission of the Chamber of Deputies (*Comisión de Vigilancia de la Auditoría Superior de la Federación*), as well as the institution's budget data. Figure 1.5 depicts the results for the ASF over a 10-year period, based on the recovery formula. For instance, for every peso allocated to the ASF in 2012, the

ASF recovered nearly 10 pesos. The overall trend for the 10-year period has been a decrease in ROI, according to this metric.

Figure 1.5. The ASF's return on investment using recoveries as a metric

Ratio of the amount of recoveries to total modified budget assigned to ASF by year

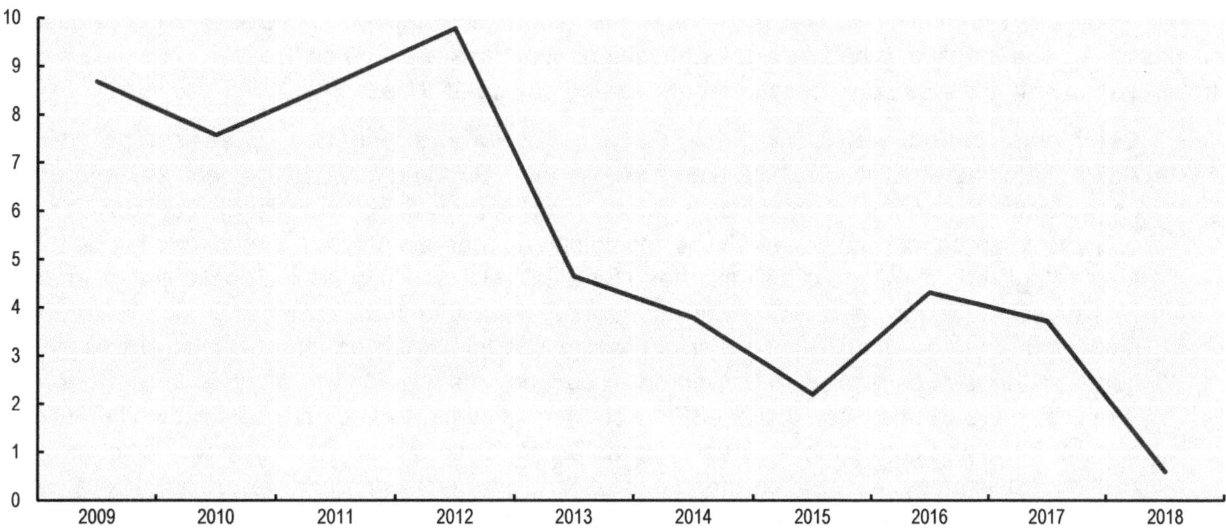

Note: The average ratio over this same period was 5.39; the median was 4.47.
Source: (OECD, 2021[28]).

The OECD's Progress Report proposed that the ASF take additional steps to assess the impact of its audit work and communicate its value, including adding new indicators to supplement its assessment of recoveries each year. Building on the proposals in that report, the ASF could also consider measuring the performance of its analytics activities. With the development of new IT capabilities in recent years, and plans for new initiatives, some of which are described in this report, the ASF will continue to invest taxpayer money in its capacity to audit effectively in a digital age. It is beyond the scope of this report to analyse all initiatives and assess metrics; however, likely costs include salaries for staff and data experts, enhancements to the IT infrastructure or architecture, license fees for software and materials for trainings. In the integrity context, the ASF could enhance its assessments to consider not only output indicators (e.g. number of irregularities detected using analytics), but also short-term outcome indicators. For example, as part of the capacity-building on follow-up processes (see Chapter 2), the DGAF could consider enhancing its data collection, in collaboration with the Specialised Anticorruption Prosecutor, to understand the ultimate impact its analytics and referrals have on the outcomes of referred cases. Much of the information, feedback and data that would support improved performance measurement can be captured in the monitoring plan described previously, and tailored for different purposes. Moreover, having a baseline for ROI can help the ASF to make decisions about new investments and scaling up successful initiatives based on evidence and results.

1.5. Summary of the proposals for action

This chapter explores considerations for the ASF to elevate analytics for assessing integrity risks at the strategic level. Setting a strategic vision, objectives and a co-ordinated course of action would help to rally all levels of the ASF around a common understanding of its use of analytics for assessing integrity risks, and can inspire a cultural shift in which auditors naturally incorporate data and analytics into all phases of the audit cycle. A strategy and action plan for analytics for integrity risk assessments would also set the tone for leadership's commitment to the professional development of auditors, while establishing a baseline for monitoring and measuring performance of investments in this area. Specifically, to advance a more strategic approach, the ASF could consider the following proposals for action:

- **Establish a unified vision for the ASF's use of data and analytics for assessing integrity risks:** Data and analytics enables teams across the ASF to achieve their objectives, and deliver on the institution's goals outlined in its strategic plan. Senior ASF officials flagged the development of a unified vision for data and analytics, including one that reflects trends related to big data, as a top strategic priority. There is a similar need for a unified vision to guide the application of analytics for assessing integrity risks. ASF's current strategy and digital transformation work programme do not emphasise this point, yet there are decentralised initiatives that have similar processes and needs in terms of capacities, skills and data requirements with long-term plans for development. Analytics plays a critical part in the ASF's work across multiple directorates, including its efforts to combat fraud and corruption. Addressing data and analytics at the strategic level, whether in the ASF's next strategy, subsequent iterations of its digital work programme, or elsewhere, would promote coherence and co-ordination across the organisation.

- **Create an action plan for analytics:** With a more coherent vision in place, the ASF could take further steps to ensure internal initiatives are aligned vertically and horizontally. The ASF's approach to analytics can be characterised as bottom-up, with specialised areas developing capacities, tools and processes that serve their individual mandates. While this model has its benefits in terms of specialisation, it also increases the risk of duplication as well as incoherent policies and procedures. The ASF could devise an action plan that focuses on institutional objectives for leveraging data and analytics to enhance audit work. A separate action plan for analytics would provide the necessary granularity for honing in on applications of data and analytics in specific areas of ASF's activities. One of these areas could be data and analytics for integrity, filling a critical gap in the attention the ASF currently pays to fraud, corruption and integrity in its strategy and digital transformation work programme.

- **Engage the National Digital Platform (*Plataforma Digital Nacional*, PDN) and the Ministry of Public Administration (*Secretaría de Función Pública*, SFP):** The shared goals of the PDN and ASF in terms of enhancing the use of data to combat corruption and detect integrity risks suggests opportunities for improved co-ordination and collaboration. The ASF could help to accelerate improvements to the platform, including addressing current gaps related to information and data from the NACS and the NAS. The ASF could also promote and support improvements to the quality of data on the PDN based on the experience of the ASF's auditors and their follow-up to certify data for audits. In turn, this could help to improve the quality of the ASF's own subsequent analysis using the PDN. Moreover, the ASF could improve co-ordination and collaboration with the SFP, including exchange of risk registries and convene regular meetings to better co-ordinate responses and outreach to the Specialised Anticorruption Prosecutor when irregularities are found.

- **Develop a plan to monitor new and existing analytics initiatives:** The ASF could develop a plan to ensure the relevance of its analytics initiatives and reliability of the results, particularly for new initiatives, in line with INTOSAI standards and international leading practices. Shifts in context, data reliability or data access can affect the accuracy and utility of various analytic techniques, including machine learning, which the ASF is developing. Continuous monitoring of the performance of the ASF's data and analytics initiatives is a critical component of the aforementioned action plan, should ASF decide to develop one. One benefit of monitoring its analytics, including the underlying models and algorithms, is that it can help the ASF to identify the extent of false positives, and understand how to refine its analytics to ensure resources and control activities are targeted appropriately. No analytics technique is fail proof, and human error can be difficult to decipher from fraud or corruption based on what essentially amounts to a review of databases. Human biases can also seep into algorithms and analyses. The monitoring plan for data and analytics can help to address such issues and provide a constructive process for the ASF to engage stakeholders in the refinement of analytical procedures.

- **Asses the return on investment of its analytics initiatives:** The OECD's *Progress Report on the Implementation of the Mexican Superior Audit of the Federation's Mandate* proposed that the ASF take additional steps to assess the impact of its audit work and communicate its value, including adding new indicators to supplement its assessment of recoveries each year. Building on the proposals in that report, the ASF could also consider measuring the performance of its analytics activities. With the development of new IT capabilities in recent years, and plans for new analytics initiatives, the ASF could enhance its assessments to consider not only output indicators, but also short-term outcome indicators. Having a baseline for return on investment (ROI) can help the ASF to make decisions about new investments and scaling up successful initiatives based on evidence and results.

References

Angel, A. (2021), "More than 80% complaints from the ASF for deviations fall in three years; impunity persists", *Animal Politico*, https://www.animalpolitico.com/2021/03/caen-denuncias-asf-desvios-impunidad-persiste/ (accessed on 17 November 2021).   [29]

ASF (2021), *Presentation by ASF Officials in the Director General of Forensic Audits, "Laboratorio de Cómputo Forense"*.   [11]

ASF (2020), *El Programa de Transformación Digital (Digital Transformation Programme)*.   [9]

ASF (2018), *2018-2026 Plan Estratégico Institucional (Strategic Institutional Plan)*, ASF.   [7]

ASF (2014), *Marco Integrado de Control Interno*, https://www.asf.gob.mx/uploads/176_Marco_Integrado_de_Control/Marco_Integrado_de_Cont_Int_leyen.pdf.   [23]

Australian National Audit Office (2020), *Corporate Plan 2020-21*, https://www.anao.gov.au/work/corporate/anao-corporate-plan-2020-21.   [10]

Cabinet Office's National Fraud Initiative, Government of the UK (2018), *Code of Data Matching Practice*, https://assets.publishing.service.gov.uk/government/uploads/system/uploads/attachment_data/file/750372/Code_of_Data_Matching_Practice.pdf.   [22]

Centre for Data Ethics and Innovation (2020), *Review into bias in algorithmic decision-making*, https://assets.publishing.service.gov.uk/government/uploads/system/uploads/attachment_data/file/957259/Review_into_bias_in_algorithmic_decision-making.pdf.   [25]

Coordination of the National Digital Strategy, Government of Mexico (2021), *Planning Process for the Development of the National Digital Strategy and Technology Policy*, https://www.gob.mx/cedn/documentos/proceso-de-planeacion-para-el-desarrollo-de-la-estrategia-digital-nacional-y-de-la-politica-tecnologica (accessed on 3 August 2021).   [4]

Executive Secretary of the National Anti-Corruption System, Mexico (2020), *The National Digital Platform: Data for the fight against corruption*, https://contralacorrupcion.mx/la-plataforma-digital-nacional/#_ftnref1 (accessed on 2 July 2021).   [18]

Government of Mexico (2021), "Diario Oficial de la Federación", in *Agreement amending, adding and repealing several provisions of the Internal Regulations of the Superior Audit Office of the Federation*.   [8]

Government of Mexico (2021), *The General Law of the National Anticorruption System (Ley General Del Sistema Nacional Anticorrupción)*, http://www.diputados.gob.mx/LeyesBiblio/pdf/LGSNA_200521.pdf.   [16]

Government of Mexico (2013), *National Digital Strategy*, https://www.gob.mx/cms/uploads/attachment/file/17083/Estrategia_Digital_Nacional.pdf.   [3]

Government of the UK (2007), *Serious Crime Act 2007*, https://www.legislation.gov.uk/ukpga/2007/27/section/49 (accessed on 3 September 2021).   [21]

INTOSAI (2019), *Data Analytics Guideline Prepared for INTOSAI's Working Group on IT Audit*.   [2]

INTOSAI (2019), *INTOSAI-P - 12 - The Value and Benefits of Supreme Audit Institutions –
making a difference to the lives of citizens*, https://www.issai.org/pronouncements/intosai-p-
12-the-value-and-benefits-of-supreme-audit-institutions-making-a-difference-to-the-lives-of-
citizens/. [26]

INTOSAI (2019), *Moscow Declaration*, https://incosai2019.ru/en/documents/46?download=275
(accessed on 3 August 2021). [6]

INTOSAI (2016), *Supreme Audit Institutions Performance Management Framework*,
https://www.idi.no/elibrary/well-governed-sais/sai-pmf/426-sai-pmf-2016-english/file. [27]

Lawyers Council for Civil and Economic Rights (2020), *Latin America Anti-Corruption
Assessment*, Cyrus R. Vance Center for International Justice and the New York City Bar,
https://www.vancecenter.org/wp-content/uploads/2021/05/Latin-America-Anticorruption-
Assessment-2020.pdf. [20]

MIT (2020), "Leading With Decision-Driven Data Analytics", *MIT Sloan Management Review*,
https://sloanreview.mit.edu/article/leading-with-decision-driven-data-analytics/ (accessed on
3 August 2021). [1]

National Anti-Corruption System (2021), *Plataforma Digital Nacional*,
https://www.plataformadigitalnacional.org/about (accessed on 5 July 2021). [17]

OECD (2021), *Progress Report on the Implementation of the Mexican Superior Audit of the
Federation's Mandate*, OECD, Paris, https://www.oecd.org/corruption/ethics/progress-report-
on-the-implementation-of%20the-Mexican-Superior-Audit-of-the-Federation-s-mandate.pdf. [28]

OECD (2019), *Follow up Report on the OECD Integrity Review of Mexico*, OECD, Paris,
https://www.oecd.org/corruption/ethics/follow-up-report-oecd-integrity-review-mexico.htm
(accessed on 3 August 2021). [19]

OECD (2019), *The Path to Becoming a Data-Driven Public Sector*, OECD Digital Government
Studies, OECD Publishing, Paris, https://doi.org/10.1787/059814a7-en. [5]

Revista do TCU (2016), "Evolution of Control in the", *Federal Court of Accounts Journal*,
http://See PDF (accessed on 3 August 2021). [15]

The European Court of Auditors (2019), "Developing data services for audit", *Presentation of
Magdalena Cordero, Director of Information, Workplace and Innovation*,
https://ecademy.eca.europa.eu/pluginfile.php/260/mod_resource/content/1/Developing%20da
ta%20services%20for%20auditors%20%E2%80%93%20the%20ECA%20experience.pdf
(accessed on 3 August 20021). [12]

UK National Audit Office (2021), *NAO strategy: progress update and estimate memorandum for
2021-22*, https://www.nao.org.uk/wp-content/uploads/2021/04/NAO-strategy-Progress-
update-and-estimate-memorandum-for-2021-22-1.pdf. [13]

UK National Audit Office (2018), *Data Analytics at the National Audit Office (UK)*,
https://www.intosaipas.org/wp-content/uploads/2020/02/Agenda-item_2A_Andy-Fisher_Data-
Analytics-at-the-UK-NAO.pdf (accessed on 3 August 2021). [14]

US Government Accountability Office (2021), *Artificial Intelligence: An Accountability Framework
for Federal Agencies and Other Entities*, https://www.gao.gov/assets/gao-21-519sp.pdf. [24]

Notes

[1] For purposes of this document, "irregularities" is used interchangeably with "integrity risks" to capture a broad set of risks related to fraud, corruption, waste, abuse and error.

[2] While this report focuses on ASF's leveraging of data and analytics for detecting irregularities, many of the issues and proposals for action raised in this report have broader implications for the ASF that can inform other analytics activities that support audits of programme performance, effectiveness and efficiency. There are tools available for the ASF to consider broader Information Technology (IT) assessments. For instance, at the time of drafting this report, the *Deutsche Gesellschaft für Internationale Zusammenarbeit* (GIZ) was developing and testing a Supreme Audit Institutions Information Technology Maturity Assessment.

[3] For instance, see the African Organisation of Supreme Audit Institutions research report on integrating big data into public sector auditing (https://afrosai-e.org.za/wp-content/uploads/2020/12/Research-Paper-Integrating-Big-Data-in-Public-Sector-Auditing.pdf); the training tool on environmental data published by the INTOSAI Working Group on Environmental Auditing (https://www.environmental-auditing.org/media/113693/23g-wgea_environmental-data_2019-fin.pdf); or the experiences of the Netherlands Court of Audit in developing an audit framework for algorithms (http://intosaijournal.org/developing-an-audit-framework-for-algorithms/).

[4] This DG was not taken into account in the OECD's analysis and drafting, as it was only established after the fact-finding mission. Therefore, the potential areas for co-ordination and risks of overlap with DGAF are not addressed in this report.

[5] The involvement of the ASF in the design, improvement and subscription to the PDN is established in Article 9, Sections XII and XIII of the General Law of the National Anticorruption System (Government of Mexico, 2021[16]).

[6] According to media reports, the FGR's success rate in terms of corruption complaints being prosecuted is low and actual convictions are non-existent. Recognising this, the ASF has adapted its strategy to reduce the number of cases referred to the FGR, while at the same time trying to improve the quality of its referrals (Angel, 2021[29]). Better data and information, including integrated information from enhanced ASF and SFP co-ordination, could help to improve the success rates of the FGR and facilitate the ASF's own strategy.

[7] The agreement with TESOFE was cancelled on 16 December 2020 by means of official letter 401-T-136/2020.

[8] At the time of writing this report, the ASF was the leader of the Working Group on Value and Benefits of SAIs.

2 Operational priorities for Mexico's supreme audit institution to enhance analytics

Data and analytics have the potential to transform the work of SAIs, but significant investment in capacity, skills and infrastructure is critical for this to happen. The ASF has already invested heavily in these areas in an effort to modernise its approach to using data and analytics. This chapter explores these issues from the perspective of the ASF's operational challenges and priorities, and in particular, issues related to improving co-ordination and analytics capacity, enhancing analytics for detecting integrity risks and nurturing a data-centric culture.

2.1. Introduction

Supreme audit institutions (SAIs) are usually data consumers that rely on other government entities for data to fulfil their mandate, which translates into the need for a broad range of expertise and knowledge about many different contexts in government and a variety of data sources. Moreover, SAIs operate in highly technological environments in which data and the means to extract value from it are constantly evolving. In this context, big data and small data alike can pose challenges for SAIs. Data and analytics have the potential to transform the work of SAIs. Examples from across the SAI community demonstrate the value they can bring to performance audits, compliance audits, financial audits and investigations. Moreover, studies suggest that investing in analytics reduces fraud. The Association of Certified Fraud Examiner's *Report to the Nations: 2020 Global Study on Occupational Fraud and Abuse* found that organisations with "proactive data monitoring and analysis" have 33 percent less fraud loss than those without it (ACFE, 2020[1]).

Nonetheless, data on its own does not have intrinsic value. It becomes an asset only when applied effectively, and this requires people, critical thinking and a learning mindset, not to mention robust information and technology (IT) infrastructure and architecture. Moreover, as described in Chapter 1, SAIs consideration of various strategic components is critical, including of their data governance framework in order to effectively take advantage of data and analytics for assessing integrity risks. In the case of Mexico's supreme audit institution, the Superior Audit of the Federation (*Auditoria Superior de la Federación*, ASF), this includes improvements to its data strategy, co-ordination and plans for continuous improvement, including assessing the impact of its efforts. These activities are also relevant outside of the integrity context. In addition to these elements, SAIs also need the capacity, expertise and infrastructure to ensure effective and efficient investment of taxpayer money in analytics. In interviews and workshops with ASF officials, addressing capacity was considered the top priority for the organisation going forward, both in terms of analysing data as well as following up on results. Officials also recognised the need for improvements to the ASF's infrastructure and availability of analytical tools or new techniques to analyse data. This chapter explores ways for the ASF to strengthen some of these operational aspects of working with data and leveraging analytics, including actions to improve co-ordination and capacity, enhance analytics for detecting integrity risks and nurture a data-centric culture.

2.2. Key systems and databases that support the ASF's analytics

As described in Chapter 1, the ASF's analytics and related processes for data governance are decentralised across different departments and teams. The Special Audit of Financial Compliance (*Auditoría Especial de Cumplimiento Financiero*, AECF) and the General Directorate of Forensic Audit (*Dirección General de Auditoría Forense*, DGAF), including DGAF's Forensic Laboratory (*Laboratorio Forense*), are key drivers of the ASF's analytics capacity. In addition, the Special Audit of Federal Spending (*Auditoría Especial de Gasto Federalizado,* AEGF*)* has developed its own capacity for managing data and carrying out analytics. The AEGF is responsible for auditing federal expenditures that are transferred to states and municipalities. Like the AECF, it consists of General Directorates (*Direcciones Generales*, DG), which have their own mandates, strategies and audit universes. As noted in Chapter 1, ASF recently introduced a new DG of Forensic Audit and Federal Spending (*Dirección General de Auditoría Forense del Gasto Federalizado, DGAFGF*) under the AEGF. The AEGF developed the System for the Control, Administration and Audit of Federal Expenditure Resources (*Sistema de Control, Administración y Fiscalización de los Recursos del Gasto Federalizado*, SiCAF).

The SiCAF is an online platform for the administration, management, monitoring and control of public works and acquisitions in states and municipalities that are financed with federalised expenditures. It facilitates auditing tenders, different phases of the procurement process and payments. It will also have geo-referenced maps of the location of public works. With the SiCAF, the AEGF also aims to enhance audit planning, promote real-time auditing and increase its territorial coverage of resources spent in states and municipalities. The AEGF will establish a permanent team to monitor registered projects and the quality of information and data inputted into the SiCAF (ASF, 2021[2]).

The COVID-19 pandemic forced the ASF to accelerate the implementation of virtual audit processes, including the SiCAF. The pandemic revealed the ASF's vulnerabilities and limitations in terms of auditors' abilities to access information and government systems in a remote environment. The SiCAF is meant to address these vulnerabilities, with the goal of allowing the ASF to audit 100 percent of public works virtually, thereby reducing the need to deploy auditors across the country. Moreover, the SiCAF will help the ASF to improve oversight throughout all phases of the project cycle. The AEGF partnered with INFOTEC, a public Mexican research centre that is part of the National Council of Science and Technology (*Consejo Nacional de Ciencia y Tecnología*, CONACYT) and specialised in the development and innovation of technological products and services. The following are key sources of data for the system to process and store information developed with INFOTEC, although not all of this information is available yet:

- The Treasury of the Federation (*Tesorería de la Federación*, TESOFE), an Administrative Unit of the Ministry of Finance and Public Credit (*Secretaría de Hacienda y Crédito Público,* SHCP) in charge of the financial management of the resources and values of the Federal Government, including: receipt of income, execution of payments charged to the expenditure budget and administration of the available resources of the TESOFE. As noted, ASF's data sharing agreement with TESOFE was cancelled in December 2020 and had not been renewed as of March 2022.
- The National Banking and Securities Commission (*Comisión Nacional Bancaria y de Valores*, CNBV), a decentralised body of the SHCP with powers of authorisation, regulation, supervision and sanction on the various sectors and entities that make up the financial system in Mexico, as well as on those individuals and legal entities that carry out activities provided for in the laws relating to the financial system. The CNBV's databases offer names of account holders and data on movements of bank accounts. As of March 2022, there was still no data sharing agreement between ASF and the CNBV.
- The Ministry of Economy (*Secretaría de Economía*, SE), a cabinet-level body responsible for economic policies and overseeing the economy, and it maintains a hotline for citizens to report suspected fraud.
- The Tax Administration Service (*Servicio de Administración Tributaria*, SAT), which maintains taxpayer records for individuals, tax vouchers, information on government suppliers, among other data.
- Unstructured data, such as audit reports and contracts. This information is not available in INFOTEC as of March 2022.
- Social media outlets (e.g. Twitter, Facebook, Instagram, YouTube and LinkedIn). This information is not available in INFOTEC as of March 2022.

According to ASF officials, the AEGF intends to complement available databases with additional information from other public institutions and that is relevant for the identification of new cases. It also intends to promote the implementation and use of software and technologies that allow the processing of unstructured information. At the time of writing this report, the lack of data sharing agreements for key databases created delays for uploading the information to servers, as noted above. Figure 2.1 provides an illustration of the system to process and store information developed with INFOTEC.

Figure 2.1. Overview of the System to process and store information developed with INFOTEC

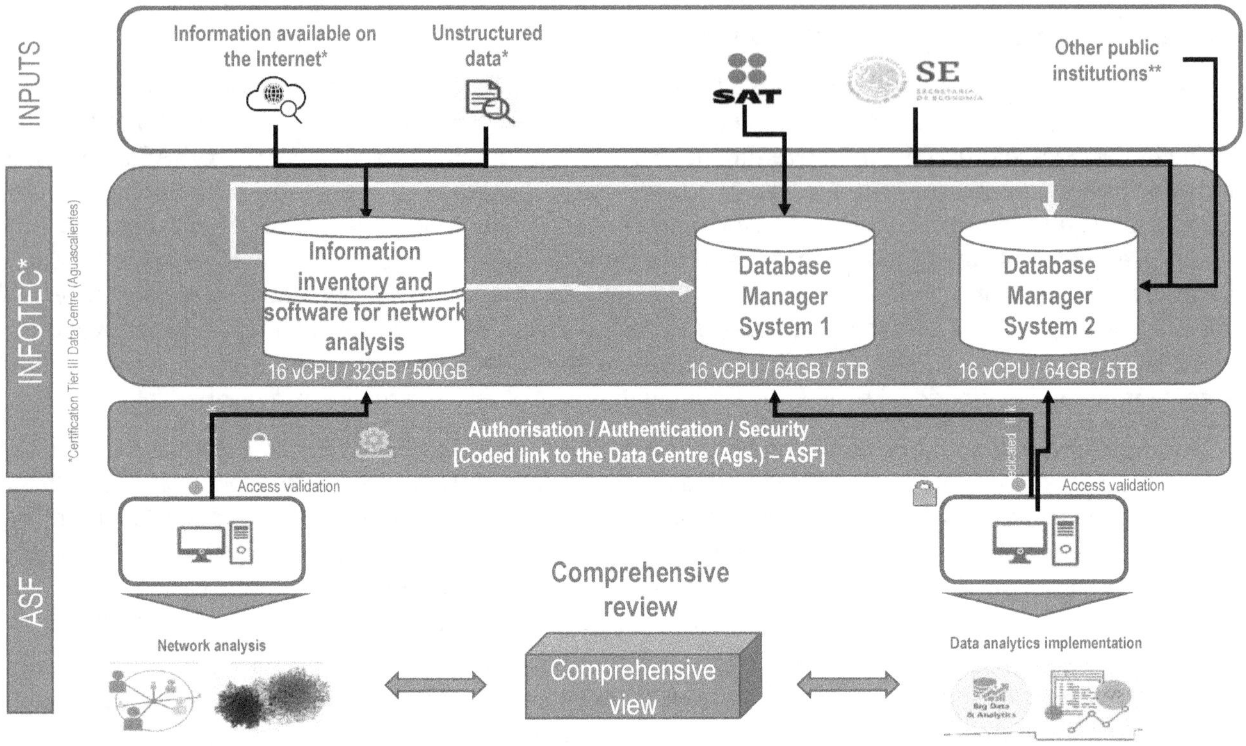

Aiming in the mid-term to:
* Advance software and technology use and implementation to allow processing such information. and
** Complement available databases with relevant additional information to identify new cases from other public institutions.

Source: ASF.

The AECF developed its own analytics capacities and an "intelligence system" (*sistema de inteligencia*) to support auditors within its department, drawing from many of the same sources as the SiCAF. The General Directorate of Audit of Information and Communications Technology (*Dirección General de Auditoría de Tecnologías de Información y Comunicaciones*, DGATIC) within the AECF is responsible for processing, storing and maintaining information, as well as setting the policies for improving the quality of data it manages. A team of three experts within the DGATIC manages the central data repository, cleaning data at the request of auditors in other DGs within the AECF, maintaining data integrity and setting data policies. The current system incorporates data from various sources, including open data sources, the ASF's own databases (e.g. data collected on government contractors), government contract databases and development bank databases.[1]

The DGATIC effectively acts as data service provider for other teams within the AECF, but it conducts some analytics on its own, such as analysis of trends or suspicious transactions in public procurement data, or analyses of sanctioned businesses. According to ASF officials, the AECF has also been developing prototypes that will allow it to add unstructured information to its database, increase its analytical capabilities and build predictive models for the integration of unstructured sources and detection of suspicious behaviour. Analytics is decentralised further to other DGs which have the subject matter expertise and use tools like Excel and ACL to support audits. The DGATIC officials described future plans for the AECF to build on its intelligence systems towards a more integrated, cloud-based system that takes advantage of other data sources, analytic techniques and outputs (e.g. visualisations and risk profiles). Like the SiCAF, this system would improve how the ASF conducts machine learning and network analysis. Figure 2.2 is ASF's own illustration of the AECF's plans for a new intelligence system, bringing together structured and unstructured data, including various forms of administrative data, into "master catalogues" of data that can ultimately be used by auditors.

Figure 2.2. Proposed new Intelligence System for the AECF

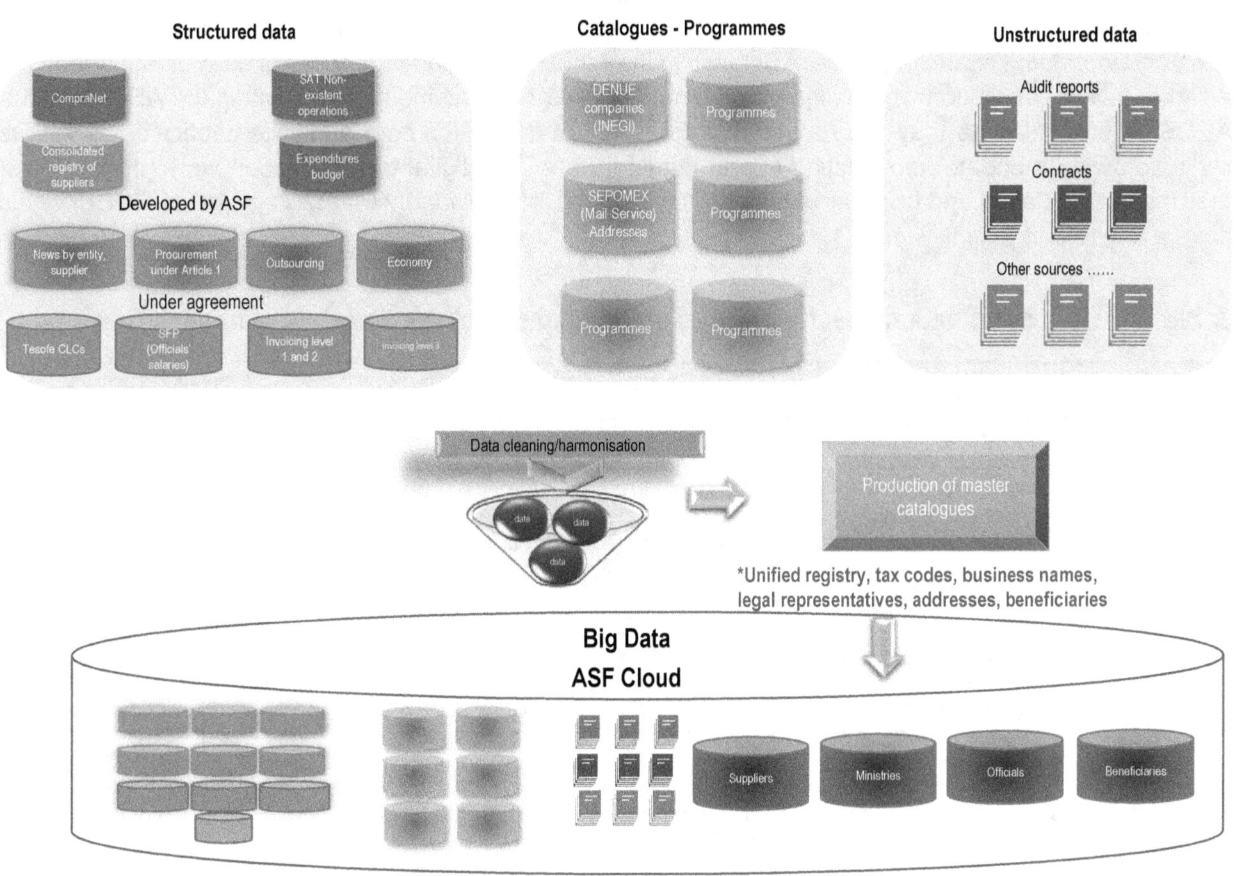

Source: (Special Audit of Financial Compliance, ASF, 2021[3]).

The ASF can access databases from other entities across the Mexican government, per national laws but this authority has its limits.[2] In particular, the ASF does not have the authority to access Platform Mexico (*Plataforma Mexico*), which is maintained by the Ministry of Public Security (*Secretaría de Seguridad y Protección Ciudadana*) and includes a number of databases consisting of police records, criminal records, biometric data, prison records and vehicle records, among other data. The ASF officials said they are working to address access issues, including limitations to other data sources, but they are often restricted due to confidentiality and national security provisions. The ASF is also exploring possibilities to license additional databases.

2.3. Improving co-ordination and building capacity

2.3.1. Strengthening internal co-ordination around data processes and analytics

There are numerous avenues for the AECF and the AEGF to enhance co-ordination, building on the existing communication as the foundation, as shown in Table 2.1. Co-ordination is an iterative process and can vary depending on the objective. As shown in the table below, higher degrees of co-ordination requires a higher level of institutional commitment on behalf of senior leadership and staff within the AECF and the AEGF, in particular, as they are responsible for much of the ASF's core analytics capacities. Given its institution-wide mandate and existing role in leading the ASF's digital transformation work programmes, the Unit of Regulation and Legislative Liaison (*Unidad de Normatividad y Enlace Legislativo*, UNEL) would have a key role to play.

Table 2.1. The co-ordination spectrum based on defined objectives and level of intensity

Co-ordination objective →	Communication	Coexistence	Co-ordinated action	Integrated action and decision making
Example of activities	Communication between the ASF's departments and teams – limited information sharing.	Joint context and capacity analysis, with actions developed partially based on the analysis (e.g. carrying out an analytics capacity gap analysis).	Joint design and/or implementation of specific activities between departments, in particular (e.g. AECF and AEGF); active partnership on an ad hoc or ongoing basis.	Consolidating various actors (departments and key general directorates) and approaches within an overall strategic framework; establishment of collaborative decision-making, monitoring and evaluation mechanisms.
Institutional commitment needed	Participation in general inter-departmental meetings; fostering informal relationships with other departments and teams in the ASF.	Participation in an ASF-wide co-ordination mechanism with a facilitated process; establishment of trust and communication required to share analyses of context (e.g. risk registries) and institutional capacity; development of limited joint decision-making capacity.	Commitment to some degree of joint decision making; senior level buy in and support.	Full transparency; senior level participation and support for achievement of common strategic objectives, and the allocation of the necessary resources.

Note: The intensity of co-ordination can be viewed on a continuum of low to high from left (starting with "Communication") to right (ending with "Integrated action and decision-making").
Source: OECD adaptation of (Strimling, 2006[4]).

In interviews with ASF officials, the AECF and the AEGF said they are aware of each other's initiatives; however, substantive co-ordination on common policies, practices or the development of tools remains limited. For instance, each department independently carries out activities related to data management, analytics and strategic planning. Moreover, the AEGF and the AECF, along with their respective DGs, have their own set of policies and processes for managing data for their audits, some of which includes databases with the same structure, even if the data fields have different information. Co-ordination occurs primarily within departments between the DGs, with limited co-ordination and co-operation between the AECF and the AEGF concerning their data and analytics efforts. According to ASF officials, part of the issue with regards data sharing is that regulations prohibit one team from accessing information of the other. Insufficient co-ordination and co-operation between the AECF and the AEGF in particular increases the risk of inefficiencies.

On the spectrum of co-ordination described above, there are several ways for the ASF to enhance internal co-ordination for improving its analytics and the data management that underlies it. Based on workshops with ASF officials, the current intensity of co-ordination is low and mostly reflects the "communication" end of the spectrum, including giving presentations on each other's initiatives and taking part in institution-wide committees. The development of an action plan for analytics would provide a constructive vehicle for advancing co-ordination beyond basic communication towards integrated action and decision making. In addition, several of the sources in the AECF's intelligence system appear to overlap with the AEGF's SiCAF, including data from SAT, SHCP, SE and TESOFE. A joint review of the extent of overlap, considering these entities have different databases, could provide assurances that there are no duplicative efforts in terms of data processing in particular. This phase, which can involve extensive data cleaning, is typically the most resource intensive, while the actual analytics makes up a smaller percentage of the time required of auditors and data experts. Figure 2.3 illustrates a general process for what is commonly referred to as "data analytics," which is often more focused on processing the "data" than doing the "analytics." Finally, according to AECF officials, many of the open source databases at its disposal are not useful, because the quality of data is poor. As a result, they prefer to organise direct access to data with the relevant authority. Improved internal co-ordination within the ASF also has the potential to reduce the burden on data owners and auditees to the extent there is a risk that multiple teams within the ASF request the same data.

Figure 2.3. Analytics as an exercise in pre-processing data

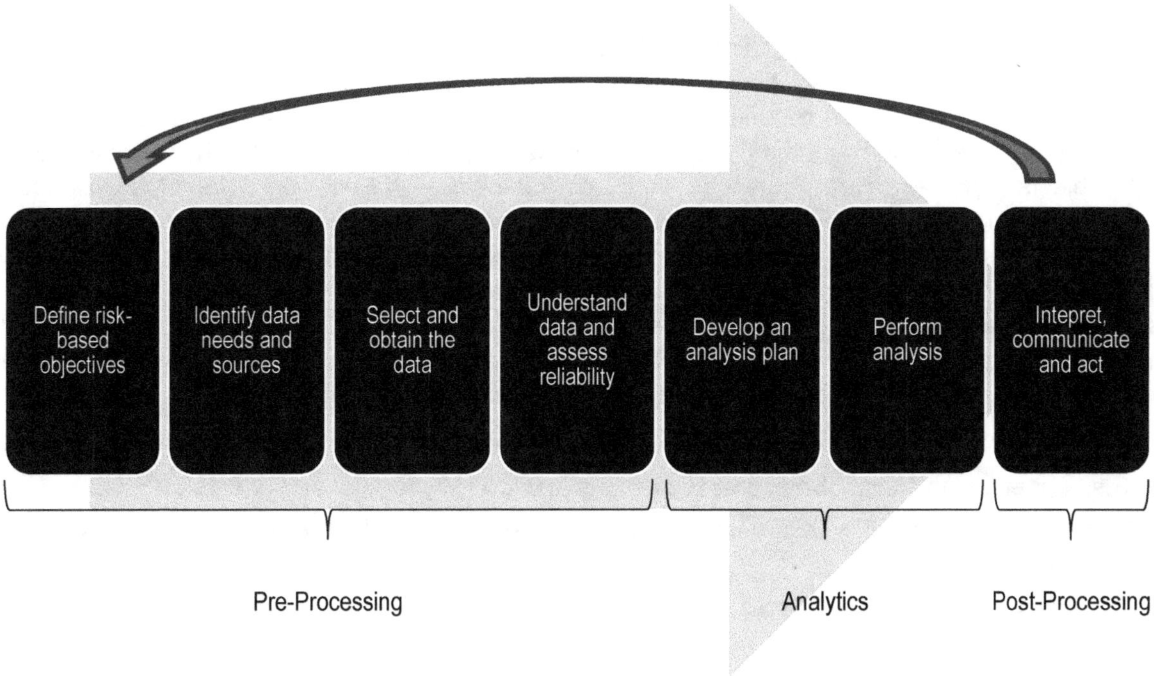

Source: (Baesens, Van Vlasselaer and Verbeke, 2015[5]).

2.3.2. Considering data sharing pilots for breaking down siloes

In interviews with the OECD, the DGATIC and the DGAF officials noted it would be useful to be able to share systems and developments in order to facilitate better co-ordination within the ASF. In the current situation, DGATIC and DGAF have limited knowledge of the databases the AEGF uses, officials said, and they recognised the possibility that the AEGF could be using a database that would help their work and vice versa. Even though the AEGF and the AECF are not able to access each other's databases by law and they have different auditees, many of the databases they use share similar structures, as noted. Moreover, the introduction of a new forensic team within AEGF (the DG of Forensic Audit and Federal Spending, or *Dirección General de Auditoría Forense del Gasto Federalizado*), suggests the possibility of furthering creating siloes of forensic activities at the directorate level. This development presents opportunities, as well as risks, in terms of data sharing or lack thereof. The ASF could consider a data sharing pilot with a discrete objective as an efficient, simple means to test collaboration. The phases of a data pilot focusing on data sharing for detecting fraud risks is depicted in Figure 2.4 and could include not only teams within the ASF, but also stakeholders and data owners outside of the ASF, such as members of the NACS, as described in the previous section.

Figure 2.4. Five phases of a data pilot for fraud detection

Source: (Commonwealth Fraud Prevention Centre, Government of Australia, 2020[6]).

Each of these phases breaks down into a series of steps to complete a data sharing pilot. In the first phase, a critical step for the ASF, there are considerations as to whether the pilot involves internal or external partners, as well as privacy and security concerns of the relevant data sources. In general, the ASF adheres to a privacy law in Mexico, the General Law on the Protection of Personal Data in Possession of Obliged Subjects (*Ley General de Protección de Datos Personales en Posesión de Sujetos Obligados*). The law governs the data sources that ASF can access, and its officials take mandatory trainings and certifications to ensure they understand the requirements. Given its mandate, the ASF has a broad authority to access data across government directly from the administration, with the exception of specific data sources. There are legal constraints for the sharing of some data (e.g. census data, data related to national security interests and private sector data). However, as illustrated by the experience of the PDN and limitations it has faced, other challenges could remain that a data sharing pilot would help to uncover:

- Cultural – this might be expressed as "we do not share data".
- Risk appetite – this might be expressed as "it is just too risky to release our data".
- Familiarity – this might be expressed as "we have never done it before, we wouldn't know where to start".
- Capability – this might be expressed as "we do not have the technical or legal expertise that we would need."
- Resources – this might be expressed as "we do not have enough resources to devote to a data sharing project" (Commonwealth Fraud Prevention Centre, Government of Australia, 2020[6]).

A data sharing pilot could help to first identify and then address these challenges constructively and incrementally, using fewer resources to test concepts before the ASF commits to more sustained forms of collaboration, such as an automated data sharing arrangement. Even if the stakeholders decide not to move ahead following the pilot, the process itself can provide insights to enhance data quality and ultimately improve fraud detection. For instance, sharing information about data sources, and if relevant, sharing responsibilities for data management, cleaning and other common activities could help to break down or prevent siloes at the auditor level. The pilot can facilitate informal channels for auditors to collaborate on data quality issues, as well as sharing data dictionaries, methodologies and techniques used, coding and even analyses to the extent they are relevant.

2.3.3. Institutionalising a cross-departmental and cross-functional capacity

Enhancing internal co-ordination between existing departments and DGs is a critical, but insufficient, step for the ASF to fulfill its own plans for developing the aforementioned IT systems, as well as advance its digital transformation work programme. Moreover, existing co-ordination mechanisms with regards to the ASF's data management and analytics are largely ad hoc, and as noted, focus largely on communication between respective departments and DGs. At a minimum, the ASF could establish a cross-functional group to formalise the current ad hoc communication and promote consistent exchange of knowledge, expertise and data across departments and DGs. The Italian Court of Audit's (*Corte dei Conti*, CdC) Data Analysis Competency Centre offers an example of this model. Box 2.1 illustrates other models from the SAIs of the United Kingdom and Turkey, both of which have recognised the need for dedicated entities with institution-wide support and responsibilities to enhance data processes and analytics.

Box 2.1. Examples of analytics communities of practice in SAIs

The United Kingdom

The United Kingdom's National Audit Office (NAO) established a Data Service to meet the demands of auditors that routinely need access to large volumes of data. This team maintains a number of large datasets, stores them in NAO's data warehouse and merges them for auditors to use and interpret. The Data Service also provides guidance for audit teams that are using the data, which can be accessed through a common Share Point site. The Methods, Economics and Statistics Hub (MESH) complements the Data Service. This community of practice leads the NAO's work on analytics and big data, and it co-ordinates across a range of specialist areas to provide training and financial support for audits and wider assurance work. In addition to data analysis and analytics, MESH's areas of expertise include economics, statistics, modelling, mapping, and qualitative analysis.

Italy

The Italian Court of Audit (*Corte dei Conti*, CdC) developed a "Data Analysis Competency Centre," which became a cross-functional team and brings together business and technical competencies to support the effective implementation of ConosCo. The Centre supports users of ConosCo to make better decisions using machine learning, analytics, predictive analysis and other data analytics techniques. This Centre is in the early stages of its development and intends to be a multi-disciplinary team with knowledge and skills that span levels of government (i.e. national and regional) as well as technologies. According to CdC officials, this effort signals a recognition that any data-driven tool is not static, and requires a capacity-building strategy to support its development and evolution.

Turkey

In 2017, the Turkish Court of Accounts (TCA) created a "Data Analysis Group" to design methodologies for using computer-assisted audit techniques (CAAT) and enhance the capability of the TCA to assess risks in municipalities. The group had other aims, including decreasing auditors' workload, analysing big data, identifying mistakes and errors in data processing, and automation of analyses to facilitate continuous monitoring. Their efforts resulted in "VERA", TCA's Data Analysis and Business Intelligence System, which automates risk analysis for over 1 400 municipalities to inform audit programming and planning.

Source: (UK National Audit Office, 2019[7]); (House of Commons, United Kingdom, 2017[8]).

The examples in Box 2.1 and the experience of other SAIs suggest that the degree of the formality of the group (e.g. working group, community of practice or unit) and its place in the ASF's hierarchy can vary based on strategic and institutional factors, including the evolution of the ASF's current analytics capacity. Decentralisation of analytics functions, as is the case in the ASF, comes with benefits. For instance, it allows teams to build expertise around specific databases and methodologies that are most relevant for their audit universe. In the context of carrying out integrity risk assessments, auditors who know the business processes of auditees can have sharper insights about the vulnerabilities in internal control systems and sources of potential integrity risks. Centralising of data management or analytics functions would not be able to replace this type of knowledge that accumulates over time.

As described in the next section, a formal data capability assessment would help the ASF to further target key issues and prioritise next steps; however, input from ASF officials already suggests that capacity gaps exist at all levels of the organisation, even though ASF has carried out trainings for a small group of auditors on big data. A community of practice that operates as a network for information exchange and knowledge sharing would be a conservative start. However, there are other ways for the ASF to go beyond communication as a form of collaboration to enhance its use of data and analytics. For instance, one model would be for the ASF to create a centralised data service or analytics function that would focus on specific cross-cutting areas of the ASF's analytics processes, while leaving the analysis to the teams. This model would be similar to the UK model of having a Data Service and the Methods, Economics and Statistics Hub, which supports auditors with training on analytics. To some extent, this approach also reflects what the AECF is already doing at the department level. Regardless of the model, given the cross-cutting nature of the ASF's data and analytics and its relevance for institution-wide goals, an effective group would likely need to be above the level of a DG and have direct reporting lines to senior leadership. It could represent a cross-section of the ASF's existing strategic and technical functions to make it distinct from existing teams, such as the UNEL and the Special Audits (i.e. the AEGF and the AECF).

The ASF could also consider establishing a formal role, such as a Chief Data Officer (CDO) or Chief Technology Officer (CTO), to act as a steward for institution-wide data policies and processes. The precise title is less important than the definition of the duties and position within the ASF hierarchy. In the current organisational structure, the UNEL exists to provide high-level advice, planning and co-ordination on the ASF's strategies for implementing IT policies and systems. While this unit provides "political governance," it is not designed to take on the operational data governance that affects the day-to-day success of the ASF's use of data, analytics or new technologies[3] that could be envisioned for a CDO- or CTO-like role. For instance, CTOs can help organisational leaders to navigate different technological options, such as clarifying specific options, trade-offs and implications, as these considerations increase in number and complexity (OECD, 2020[9]). The CDO can act as a general caretaker of data, responsible and accountable for all of the ASF's information assets, including processes around generating data and ensuring their quality and security (Stockpoll, 2021[10]). In some SAIs, an Innovation Lab fulfils some of these roles, as described in the section on experimentation.

The CDO or the CTO role is not always filled by the same person. However, the entity requires the authority and autonomy to provide vision and visibility across the ASF, as well as authority to make strategic investments in architecture, software and tools to address institution-wide needs and priorities. Direct reporting lines to the Auditor General facilitates this role. The individual does not necessarily have to have a technical background in auditing, but would have a grounding in data management and new technologies to play an operational role within the ASF. The Office of the Comptroller and Auditor General of India describes a similar role for its Centre for Data Management and Analytics (CDMA) as follows:

> *CDMA will play an advisory and supporting role for the overall use of data analytics…CDMA will facilitate through capacity building, collecting third party data at the central level, identifying new software, assessing applicability of different analytic techniques/analytic models, and disseminating them in IA&AD. CDMA will provide technical support to the field offices in their data analytic efforts wherever necessary. The Data Analytic models will be vetted and approved by CDMA, in consultation with functional wings in headquarters (Office of the Comptroller and Auditor General of India, 2017[11]).*

Hiring a CDO, CTO, or data scientists does not automatically translate into an ability to extract value from data, or leverage analytics to enhance detection of integrity risks. Digital transformation from an operational perspective relies on a team of individuals that bring the right mix of skills and knowledge. As discussed, this includes individuals with expertise in fraud and corruption to the extent the objectives of the analytics function is to enhance detection of these risks. Given the rapid rate at which fraud detection practices are evolving, the roles of audit institutions are shifting beyond just conventional audits, especially as a result of the COVID-19 pandemic, The onboarding of individuals with a strong understanding of data and analytics is critical, but many SAIs have turned to co-sourcing, contracting, or outsourcing models, which can provide additional expertise to the department or its projects. Regardless of the approach, the ASF can enhance the cross-functionality of its teams as it further develops its capacities for using data, analytics and new technologies. Figure 2.5 illustrates the key elements of a cross-functional team from the perspective of the European Court of Auditors.

Figure 2.5. Key elements of a cross-functional and data-driven audit team

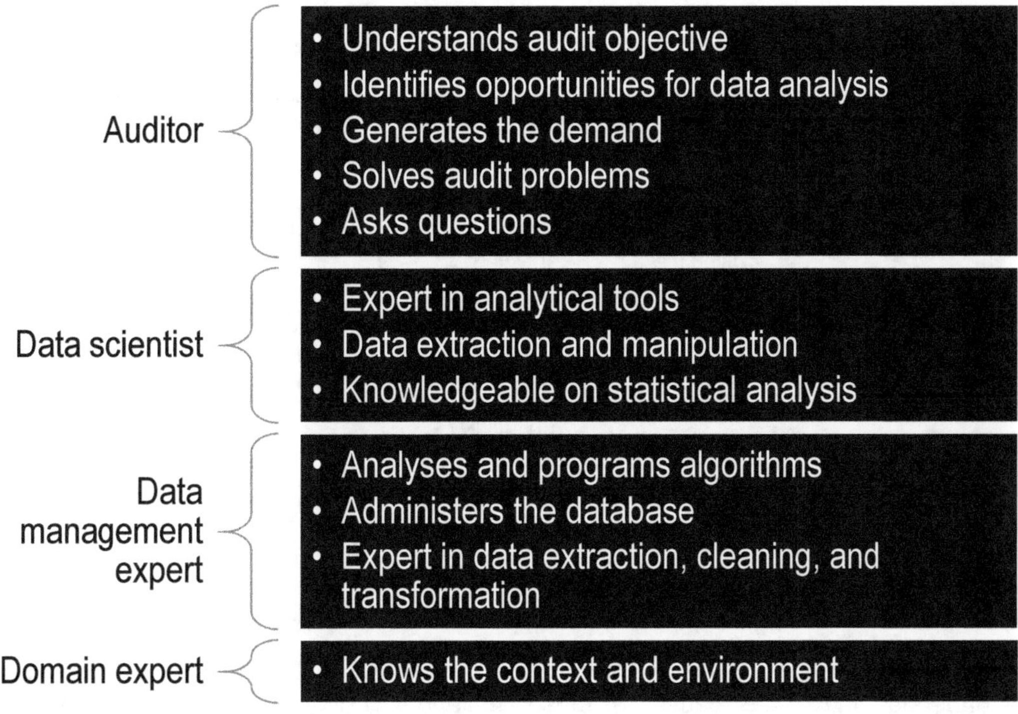

Source: (The European Court of Auditors, 2019[12]).

2.3.4. *Conducting an internal assessment to further explore capacity gaps and data capabilities*

The proposals for action above reflect some of the key priorities for the ASF to enhance its current approach to data management and analytics, drawing primarily from responses to a questionnaire, as well as interviews and workshops with ASF officials. These inputs offer a useful starting point; however, they focused on the analytics led by select departments and by design were not meant to cover the broad scope of issues facing the ASF concerning data and analytics. The ASF could take additional steps to elaborate on its internal capacity challenges within all departments and teams, including an institution-wide assessment of capacity gaps. According to the International Organisation of Supreme Audit Institution (INTOSAI) Development Initiative's *Strategic Management Handbook for SAIs*, assessments can be carried out as a step in strategy development, so that capacity gaps are determined in relation to defined objectives and outputs (INTOSAI, 2020[13]). For example, the ASF could start with its objectives for enhancing the use of data and analytics in its audits and investigations, and addressing issues of operational data governance, as described above. The linkage to concrete objectives will help the ASF to nuance the assessment so that it targets gaps that are relevant for what the ASF wants to do in the future, while recognising the diversity of needs across the organisation. As discussed, the ASF's current analytics capacity is highly decentralised and operates in silos, so any capacity assessment would need high level stewardship to ensure collaboration between departments, particularly the AECF and the AEGF.

There are numerous frameworks available to support the ASF in carrying out an assessment of its internal capacity for data and analytics. Effective assessments map the key elements of data governance particularly capacity for coherent implementation, as described in Chapter 1. Assessments often provide a holistic view of gaps and strengths as a basis for establishing development priorities. In New Zealand, the government developed a data capability framework that defines 25 capabilities for effective data use, based on seven categories of the data lifecycle (see Figure 2.6). The ASF could reference this framework as a template for identifying potential areas of improvement with respect to strategic planning, performance development, recruitment and on boarding (Government of New Zealand, 2020[14]).

Figure 2.6. Data capability framework of the New Zealand government

Plan	Collect	Describe	Store	Analyse	Use	Save/Destroy
The processes and resources are mapped out for the lifecycle of the data. The project's goals are stated, and a full data plan is created.	The data is gathered or generated by the individuals/ organisations wanting to use it.	The data is accurately described using the appropriate metadata standards.	The data is stored in a digital repository, and is made secure and reusable (often this very quickly follows collection).	The data is analysed/ i.e. it is explored and interpreted.	The data is used for the purpose for which it was collected/ generated and reused for additional value.	Actions are taken to safeguard the long-term viability and availability of the data.

Source: (Government of New Zealand, 2020[14]).

New Zealand's data capability assessment focuses on breadth over depth, but it will not necessarily offer a greater understanding of root causes of those challenges. For a more comprehensive and nuanced picture, the ASF could conduct a root cause analysis that would provide further insights about not only the technical challenges facing auditors, but also the human and cultural elements that influence the ability of the ASF to adopt analytics and fulfil broader goals of digital transformation. As part of this analysis, the ASF could also look at specific challenges facing individual teams and processes, including those related to the application of analytics for detecting irregularities and integrity risks.

SAIs use root cause analysis for their own audits in an effort to go beyond the identification of deficiencies and understand the key challenges and features of an issue. For instance, the Auditor-General of South Africa in its Consolidated General Report on National and Provincial Audit Outcomes provides an overview of how auditees have addressed the root causes of audit findings (Auditor General South Africa, 2020[15]). In addition, the INTOSAI Development Initiative, a not-for-profit organisation that supports SAIs to enhance their performance and capacity, promotes the use of root cause analysis in its implementation handbooks for International Standards of Supreme Audit Institutions (ISSAIs) for performance and compliance auditing, and provides guidance on different approaches.[4] Box 2.2 offers additional insights and a resource for conducting root cause analyses from the Canadian Audit and Accountability Foundation. These references could support the ASF in applying a root cause analysis internally to obtain a fuller understanding of its capacity challenges for using data and analytics. This analysis can complement the proposals for action in Chapter 1 to enhance the ASF's strategic approach to analytics and create an action plan, with performance monitoring, so that further assessment of capacity and resource issues are tied to actual institution-wide objectives.

Box 2.2. Guidance for conducting root cause analysis

The Canadian Audit and Accountability Foundation (CAAF) is a not-for-profit organisation dedicated to promoting and strengthening public sector performance audit, oversight, and accountability in Canada and abroad. Per the CAAF, root cause analysis can be an effective approach for helping government entities understand complex challenges and fundamental areas of concern. By focusing on the principle question – "why?" we may better be able to identify systemic deep-seeded issues faced by the organisation. Root cause analysis can be integrated into every step of the auditing process—planning, examining and reporting, as shown in Figure 2.7.

Figure 2.7. Canadian Audit and Accountability Foundation's Use of Root Cause Analysis and Audits

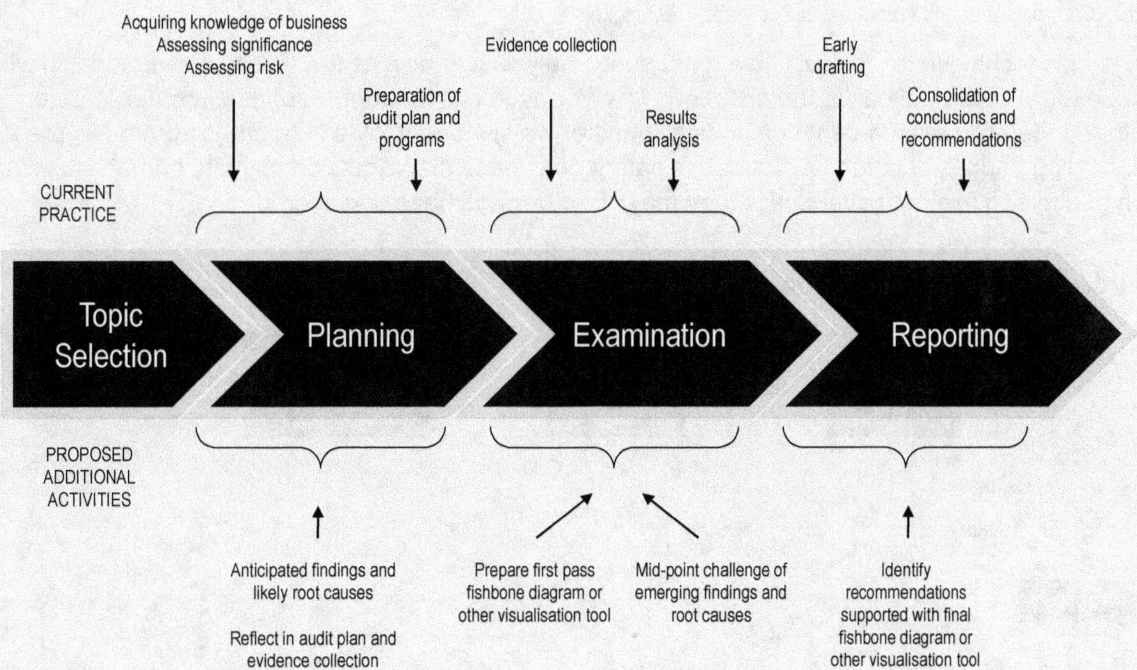

Source: (Canadian Audit and Accountability Foundation, 2020[16]).

Root causes are often governance-related or operations-related. The first pertains to overarching structures, strategy and oversight. The second is more concerned with the daily workings of the organisation. Increasingly as well, auditors also see broader organisational culture as a third potential category of root causes, and have begun to develop more rigorous methods by which to monitor this phenomenon. Figure 2.8 shows some of the most frequently observed root causes.

Figure 2.8. Canadian Audit and Accountability Foundation's Main Areas of Potential Root Causes

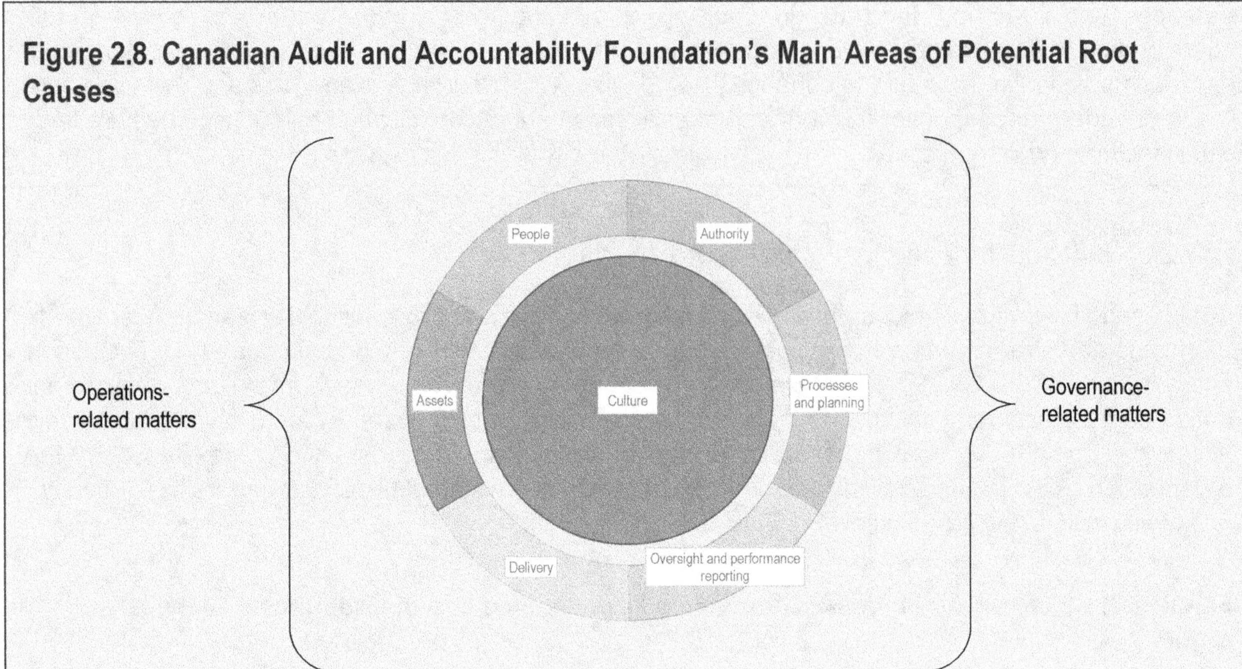

Source: (Canadian Audit and Accountability Foundation, 2020[16]).

One simple technique for conducting a root cause analysis is known as the "five whys" method, in which the auditor(s) repeatedly asks the question "why" for each subsequent response in order to determine the true underlying reason behind a finding. Another way is to employ a fishbone diagram (Figure 2.9). By including nudges of potential root cause categories, these diagrams can mitigate human biases and push auditors to think of novel topics they may not otherwise have considered.

Figure 2.9. A Fishbone Diagram

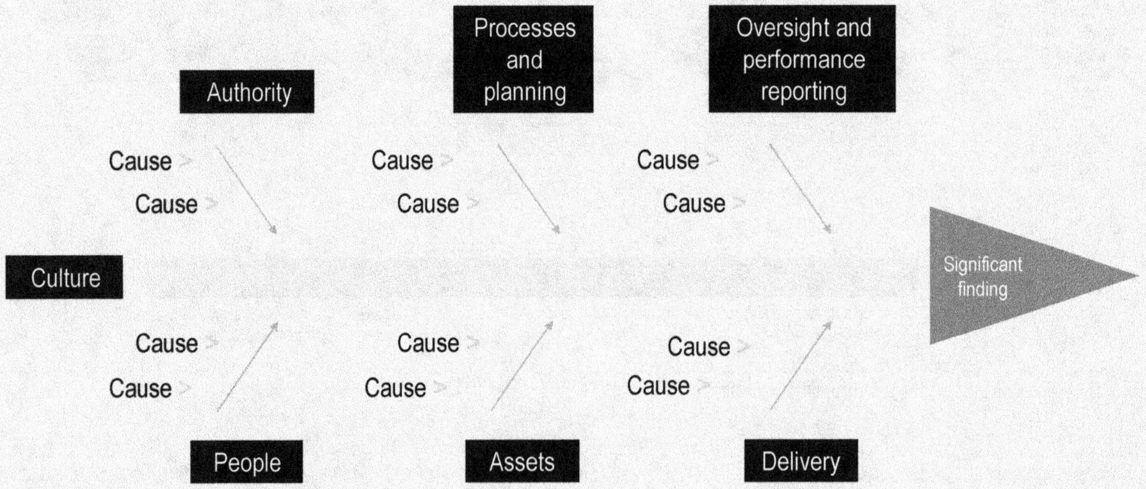

Source: (Canadian Audit and Accountability Foundation, 2020[16]).

2.4. Enhancing analytics for detecting integrity risks

2.4.1. Improving analysis of risk trends and use of dashboards

Many of the strategic considerations and operational priorities discussed above, while having broader implications for the ASF's digital transformation, influence its ability to leverage data for detecting integrity risks. Responses from ASF officials in questionnaires and interviews highlighted several specific priorities to enhance the tools and processes in place for applying analytics to the detection of integrity risks, including the development of a risk dashboard to improve how the ASF tracks, visualises and communicates risks across the organisation. According to ASF officials, while the systems envisioned by the AEGF and AECF incorporate dashboards, the ASF has yet to develop a dashboard for supporting its risk analytics for irregularities. SAIs have long used dashboards to support risk identification and tracking. Developing a dashboard, incorporating insights and data from the DGAF in particular, would be a low cost and high return approach to facilitate sharing of risk data and facilitate auditors' analyses.

As noted in interviews with ASF officials, within the AECF, the DGAF and the Forensic Laboratory support other teams in identifying irregularities and potential fraud, and they maintain a risk registry with red flags. The registry is effectively a database for uploading findings and information corresponding to specific audits with an explanation of the irregularity detected. It includes a brief description of the evidence for the irregularity or potential fraud. Currently, the risk information is communicated ad hoc during meetings among a group of DGs and relevant work teams. The meetings cover a range of issues, including red flags. Risks are also shared across the organisation in the context of specific audits. For instance, DGs may detect an irregularity during the course of their audits, in which case they would engage the DGAF to conduct forensic analyses or investigations, as needed. Among other databases at its disposal, officials said the DGAF is also developing a database that includes the companies flagged for irregularities in prior audits as a resource for future audit teams to identify past issues.

As discussed in meetings with the OECD, the DGAF officials noted the use of the registry and informal database of risks could be enhanced, for instance, by analysing trends and patterns of risks in the data. A risk dashboard offers a vehicle for disseminating such analyses, while allowing auditors themselves to access and explore the information that the DGAF maintains to support audits. Moreover, the use of dashboards can be useful for continuous monitoring and providing auditors with off-the-shelf or automated tools to conduct analyses and prioritise risks. Visualisations incorporated into dashboards can also help auditors to analyse entire datasets for outliers and potential irregularities. The new systems of the AEGF and AECF both envision such functionalities. Box 2.3 shows how the Turkish Court of Account made use of risk dashboards and automated trend analysis to support its annual audit programming.

Box 2.3. Automating risk analyses at the Turkish Court of Accounts

The Turkish Court of Accounts (TCA) created "VERA", a Data Analysis and Business Intelligence System, which automates risk analysis for over 1 400 municipalities to inform audit programming and planning. VERA provides auditees a standard, automated tool for risk-based ranking of over 1 400 municipalities. VERA allows management to take into account risks before the TCA's annual audit programming and supports the creation of the audit strategy. In addition, auditors use the results of the risk analyses to plan audits, as well as identify possible material misstatements in financial reports that could represent errors and fraud. All auditors have access to VERA, and are able to assess the results of VERA's automated analyses related to risks and financial indicators in a dashboard or automatically generated reports.

Source: Interview with the OECD.

In addition, the experience of the UK National Audit Office (NAO) demonstrates that investing in dashboards and off-the shelf tools for auditors can also have benefits for reporting. The NAO's Data Service has developed various tools for its auditors, such as web-scraping of inspection reports to harvest data on school funding or to assess the readability of tax guidance, which automate phases of the analytic process. This allows auditors to spend more time analysing information and data, and less time collecting it. The visualisations offered on the NAO's dashboard not only support analyses, but they can also be integrated into reports to raise attention about issues and support key messages. Some visualisations can attract as much attention as the report itself (UK National Audit Office, 2018[17]).

2.4.2. Enhancing follow-up on findings and creating feedback loops to improve analytics

At the conclusion of its audits, the DGAF lays out its "determination of the facts" for the auditee, which has 30 working days to resolve the findings before the ASF issues a report or presents a complaint to the National Prosecutor's Office (*Fiscalía General de la República*, FGR). Only in cases when it is clear a crime has been committed can ASF issue a report to relevant authorities, before the end of this 30-day period. If the DGAF identifies evidence of fraud or corruption, in accordance with the *Law on Auditing and Accountability* (*Ley de Fiscalización y Rendición de Cuentas de la Federación*) and in compliance with the ASF's internal regulations, it must prepare technical reports, which are sent to the Legal General Directorate for referring to relevant authorities. The DGAF relies on co-ordination with the Special Audit of Monitoring, Reporting and Investigation (*Auditoría Especial de Seguimiento, Informes e Investigación*, AESII) and the AECF for follow-up of audits, as its authority ends with the issuing of its findings.[5]

Follow-up is a fundamental phase of the audit process, reflected in various INTOSAI standards and guidance.[6] SAIs can evaluate impact in different ways, including assessing the impact and the uptake of its recommendations by auditees (EUROSAI, 2019[18]). ASF institutionalised a follow-up mechanism in the AESII; however, according to officials, the team is under-resourced and follow up can be lengthy. Knowing the status and the outcome of audits is a critical step in the feedback loop for the DGAF and other DGs. For example, feedback loops—knowing the results of audits and how the DGAF's findings supported outcomes—act as a control for the DGAF's and Forensic Laboratory's own analytics functions. The DGAF can fine tune its forensic methodologies and analytics based on the ultimate results of the audits and whether findings led to concrete actions. Optimisation of methodologies helps to reduce false positives and false negatives, and enhance the logic that underlies algorithms and indicators for detecting irregularities.

2.4.3. Strengthening analysis of unstructured and semi-structured data

Improving the management, processing and analyses of unstructured data has become a key priority for many SAIs to enhance its analytics in the digital age. By some estimates, including a 2016 study on text mining, unstructured or semi-structured data accounts for over 80 percent of all data (Talib et al., 2016[19]). Unstructured and semi-structured data accounts for large amounts of "big data" and will be an ongoing challenge for the ASF in the future. The AEGF and the AECF both envision improvements over the coming years in terms of the ASF's architecture, methodologies and tools (e.g. machine learning) to better analyse "big data." In interviews, ASF officials emphasised the need to build capacity to achieve its ambitious goals in this area, which will necessarily require improvements to how the ASF manages, processes and analyses unstructured and semi-structured data.[7] They also highlighted the need for improving capacity for managing and analysing unstructured data as one of their top priorities in the coming years.

Other initiatives have the potential to lead to the systematic collection of more unstructured data than the ASF has ever had to manage in the past. For instance, the ASF recently established a Digital Mailbox (*Buzón Digital*) to enhance the bilateral communication between auditors and auditees. This platform allows the ASF and audited entities to manage the audit process electronically, such as by sending requests and certifying documents. It will also facilitate the auditees' submission of documentation for audits, allowing the ASF to collect text files and supporting evidence for audit easier than it has ever been able to in the past. Moreover, as noted, the ASF has also developed prototypes to add unstructured information to existing databases, which in turn would help building predictive models, detecting suspect behaviour and increasing analytics capabilities.

The systematisation and digitalisation of this process makes auditing easier and promotes efficiencies, particularly in a remote environment, but it comes with risk. One risk is that auditees will submit more documentation, even if it is irrelevant for the audit, which would have the potential to overwhelm the audit team unless they have the appropriate tools and skills to analyse the text quickly. Text mining and other analytic techniques can be helpful in such situations, depending on the objectives of the audit and the format of the evidence submitted. There are several examples of SAIs that have progressed in recent years in their capacity to process and analyse unstructured data. Many of these initiatives focus on one type of analytic technique, and it is common to see examples that focus on text data. For instance, the SAI of Germany, the *Bundesrechnungshof*, analysed how federal government entities communicated to the public and its impact on public perception and the readability of messages. To do this, the SAI explored the use of various analytic techniques, including web-scraping, text mining, natural language processing and sentiment analysis of publicly-available sources (e.g. press releases, social media posts and news articles) (EUROSAI, 2021[20]).

Similar processes can be used in the context of assessing corruption risks in infrastructure. For example, a line ministry could assess internal risks of fraud or corruption by scraping emails or social media to identify red flags, like key words or evidence of procurement officials spending beyond their means. To maximise the value of text analytics, entities may use the fraud triangle as a reference to develop a list of keywords based on the industry, relevant fraud risks, and data set (OECD, 2019[21]). Social network analysis is also commonly applied to unstructured data related to infrastructure and public procurement in order to identify collusion amongst actors in the procurement cycle. Applying network analysis in this context can help to raise red flags and identify corruption risks. Moreover, data visualisations can be used to present the results of network analysis to identify "hot spots" of potential fraudulent activity.

The ASF could further develop its own capacity to analyse unstructured and semi-structured data, building on current initiatives Figure 2.10 provides a broader framework for the ASF to take into consideration when thinking about a strategic approach to unstructured/semi-structured data that goes beyond text analytics, and accounts for the different types of unstructured data sources it encounters, including audio, images and video. Going beyond text data, the framework could be useful for the DGAF and teams that collect other types of unstructured and semi-structured data.

Figure 2.10. A framework for capturing and analysing unstructured data

Data acquisition			Preprocessing	Processing	Analytics/Output		
Unstructured or semi-structured data API		Textual data	Metadata extraction, tagging, stemming, tokenisation, stop words removal	Feature selection, term frequency, document term matrix	Segment doc classification, named entry recog., information retrieval, concept extraction, topic modelling	Enterprise service bus (ESB)	KMS, BI Dashboards
		Audio	Preprocessing, sorting audio signals	Parametric feature extraction (pitch, energy, intensity), pattern classification, audio segmentation	Trend analysis, quality assurance, root cause analysis, emotion detection, talk analysis		
		Visual	Image resizing, conrast adjustment, CLAHE, histogram eq., quantisation	Edge detection, shape detection, active region, segmentation, feature extraction	Sentiment analysis, image classification, facial recognition, object segmentation, object localisation, object detection		
		Video	SIFT descriptors, feature extration, feature fusion	Contrast adjustment, speech transcription, key frame extraction	Trend analysis, sentiment analysis, event classification, topic modelling, object detection, facial recognition		

Source: (Onwujekwe, Ngwum and Osei-Bryson, 2020[22]).

The various processing and analytic techniques described in the figure above are beyond the scope of this report; however, the diversity of techniques and their underlying tools highlight the need for the ASF to consider strategically how to approach unstructured data. As noted above, this starts with defining clear objectives and priorities of auditors, while building capacities based on further assessment in the gaps in capabilities. Many of the analytics described are those that the ASF, particularly DGAF, may already be carrying out. However, as shown in Figure 2.10, the process of integrating findings and results from the analysis of unstructured data into the traditional systems of the ASF, as well as into dashboards for auditors to reference, still largely remains an ambition for future work.

2.5. Nurturing a data-centric culture

2.5.1. Promoting digital skills and ethical use of data through trainings

Introducing new systems or tools is insufficient; developing skills, motivation and interest in analytic approaches is vital for sustaining future analytics initiatives. Leading practices from other SAIs consistently highlight the development of auditors' skills and capabilities as a key enabler of digital transformation. For instance, the National Audit Office of Finland's (NAOF) maturity in terms of data and analytics reflects the ASF's own path, as it advances with its digital transformation work programme and updates its architecture and tools to better support auditors. Officials from the NAOF described the next phase of their digital transformation as one in which data and analytics becomes more systematised and integrated across the NAOF's audit work. In discussions with the OECD and the ASF, NAOF officials highlighted people, skills and organisational culture as key enablers on its digital journey. Officials also highlighted the need to focus on building a culture and models for continuous process development, driven by the audit expertise, the availability of data and opportunities of new technologies (Kärki and Saarteinen, 2020[23]).

Data literacy is often highlighted as a key requirement of modern auditors' skillset, as described, and is the focus of trainings, workshops and guidance for SAIs. While critical, data literacy—the ability to read, interpret, create and communicate data as information (OECD, 2020[24])—is just one component of a broader set of competencies that the ASF could focus on in developing its workforce to meet the demands of auditing in a digital age. In addition to data literacy, the ASF could promote the development of digital skills, defined as the broader range of abilities to use digital devices, communication applications, and networks to access and manage information. For auditors, these skills include an understanding of software, tools and data (OECD, 2020[24]).

The distinction between data literacy and having digital skills reflects the notion that auditors have different specialities and require varying levels of specialisation when it comes to managing and using data; however, all auditors can benefit from having an understanding and fluency with a range of digital tools and technologies that are critical for the modern auditing profession. Auditors with digital skills are data literate, but they are also equipped to ask strategic questions, understand limitations of techniques and tools and maintain realistic expectations about time and resources when planning the use of data and deciding on methodological trade-offs. At the time of drafting this report, officials said ASF had trained 50 auditors on the use of "big data," but without elaborating on the details of the content or target audience for the trainings.

Nonetheless, when thinking about the competencies needed for its auditors, the ASF could draw inspiration from the European Union's Digital Competence Framework (DigComp), which is a tool to improve citizen's digital competence. In its report, *Building digital workforce capacity and skills for data-intensive science,* the OECD assessed the relevance and adequacy of DigComp for the academic science community. As a type of evaluator, external auditors in the public sector share many of the same requirements as academics in terms of digital competencies. Moreover, the ASF could follow many of the same principles of the science community reflected below, including the promotion of transparency and leading by example (i.e. protecting one's reputation). The criteria below, which include both the OECD's additions to the DigComp's original framework as well as elements of the original framework itself, can provide a useful categorisation for the ASF as it considers the types of digital skills its auditors need in addition to digital literacy:

- Information and digital literacy: Browsing, searching and filtering data; critically evaluating credibility and reliability of data sources; organising and storing data. Understanding of statistics to help evaluation and analysis of data; understanding of requirements for reproducibility.

- Communication and collaboration: Sharing data; knowing about referencing and attribution practices; using digital tools and technologies for collaborative processes; protecting one's reputation. Following open science principles to share data, information and content, engage in good digital citizenship, and improve collaboration; extend knowledge of referencing and attribution practices to research data and software citation/referencing; protecting academic reputation, both of one's own organisation and that of academic research more generally.

- Digital content creation: Creating new, original and relevant content and knowledge; understanding copyrights and licenses; programming and software development, visualisation of data and information to convey knowledge.

- Safety: Protecting personal data, protection of sensitive data, understanding of tools and techniques such as delinking, anonymisation and safe heavens.

- Problem solving: Customising digital environments to personal needs; using digital tools to create knowledge and innovate processes; identifying digital competence gaps and seeking opportunities for self-improvement (OECD, 2020[25]).

The "safety" competency touches on a critical issue for the ASF and SAIs that goes beyond the competencies described above. This involves the ethical implications of data use, including auditors' own use of data. For this purpose, and depending on their position and level of responsibility, the ASF could consider this competency beyond what is described in the framework above. There are several ways the ASF can raise awareness and promote the ethical use of data. Box 2.4 provides examples from the OECD's *Good Practice Principles for Data Ethics in the Public Sector*.

Box 2.4. Good practices for promoting the ethical use of data

The *Good Practice Principles for Data Ethics in the Public Sector* shed light on the value and practical implications of data ethics in the public sector. They aim to support public officials in the implementation of data ethics in digital government projects, products, and services so that: i) trust is placed at the core of their design and delivery; and ii) public integrity is upheld through specific actions taken by governments, public organisations and, at a more granular level, public officials.

The Thematic Group on Data-driven Public Sector, meeting under the aegis of the OECD Working Party of Senior Digital Government Officials (E-leaders), drew together *Good Practice Principles for Data Ethics in the Public Sector*. They emerge from observed practices in digital government and data-driven public sectors across OECD Member and non-Member countries. The following good practices provide insights as to how organisations can promote the ethical use of data:

- Ensure the availability of multi-faceted and diverse teams working on or collaborating around specific projects. Diversity in the workplace can help to mitigate biases by offering multiple perspectives on a policy issue and fostering inclusive and informed decisions in terms of the data informing or resulting from a project (e.g. selection of data sources, data availability issues, data access restrictions, data's reflection of reality).

- Publish data governance and management policies, practices, and procedures, especially around the use of personal data.

- Engage in social dialogue with relevant actors inside and outside the public sector. These include actors whose data is being used, or their representatives, and secondary stakeholders who can be affected or harmed by data use. Multi-stakeholder and multi-faceted approaches can help in identifying risks, defining boundaries and channelling actions prior, during and after the deployment of projects, policies and decisions involving the access to, sharing and use of data.

- Communicate to relevant stakeholders, or their representatives, in a clear and understandable way about the role of data (e.g. expected benefits and trade-offs), and its primary purpose – including in the context of training algorithms. Intention and use beyond the original purpose and the impact of not consenting to data use should also be communicated (e.g. delays due to slower decision-making procedures to grant access to or deliver public services).

- Acknowledge the social context, including factors such as the presence of indigenous communities and native nonofficial languages to foster inclusion.

- Educate relevant stakeholders (e.g. data subjects and their representatives, and those from vulnerable, underrepresented, or marginalised groups in society) on data governance, including its meaning and implications for them. Confront scenarios in which only privileged and educated segments of the population have a voice and say in how their data is being used. This includes the capacity to contest certain uses of data.

Source: (OECD, 2020[24]).

2.5.2. *Creating room for experimentation and small wins*

Among SAIs with successful initiatives to incorporate data and analytics into their audit work, an openness to experimentation is a consistent theme, even when other aspects of the SAI's work and culture remain risk averse. ASF has demonstrated a willingness to experiment. For instance, ASF officials said the AEGF launched a pilot exercise whereby the audit areas were provided with cases of suspicious suppliers and contractors, so that they could be reviewed in greater detail during audits. The auditors' feedback from this effort will be used to improve ASF's analytics and establish guidelines to extend the use of data in more audits.

As noted in Chapter 1, leadership can make its support for strategic experimentation explicit in its strategy and action plan for analytics, for instance. The freedom for auditors to experiment creates opportunities for both small wins and small losses, meaning a SAI can pilot new methodologies, tools and data sources in a controlled and cost-efficient way before deciding whether to scale up or avoid developing further. For SAIs with "Innovation Labs," experimentation has become a strategic objective. One benefit of an innovation lab is that it helps to institutionalise knowledge and expertise, and for the ASF, it could help to advance new methodologies it is already considering that may benefit multiple departments. This would be a key difference from the ASF's existing analytics efforts, including the DGAF's Forensic Laboratory, which focuses more on supporting investigative processes for a specific directorate, rather than promoting institution-wide innovation as a priority with benefits for integrity risk detection and beyond. The Office of the Auditor General of Norway (OAGN) established an innovation lab to promote data science within the OAGN and support auditors with a range of tools and functions (see Box 2.5).

Box 2.5. The Innovation Lab at the Office of the Auditor General of Norway

The Office of the Auditor General of Norway created the Innovation Lab in 2019 as a semi-autonomous body to advance the use of data science, machine learning and provide the country's audit work with more computing power. The lab conducts a broad scope of work, including:

- gathering and preparing data for audits
- conducting analytics work on demand
- creating applications to make the work of auditors more efficient
- educating auditors about the use of machine learning
- experimenting with new analytics techniques
- promoting a culture of data science across the organisation.

The Innovation Lab has found success as a result of being given the freedom to experiment, receiving full support from management, and using free open-source technology to reduce costs. The group hires auditors rather than individuals with technology backgrounds and for most of its work, focuses on finding solutions to long-standing root cause concerns. By solving some of the concrete problems faced by auditors, they have built credibility and trust across the OAGN, and by managing the data sciences, the office gives auditors more time to focus on analysis.

Source: (Office of the Auditor General of Norway, 2021[26]); (OAGN Innovation Lab, 2020[27]).

Establishing an Innovation Lab or adding a permanent team to the ASF's organisational chart is not the only approach. Moreover, the ASF's existing teams demonstrate a high level of ambition to innovate, as illustrated by some of the examples described in this report. Nonetheless, in conversations with ASF officials, the notion of experimentation and investing resources in pilots before investing in the overhaul of architecture or introduction of new tools was not part of the strategic approach. Considering the ASF's current structure and initiatives, the ASF could also consider temporary models to tap into the skills and innovative energy of its staff. For instance, the Auditor General of Wales developed a 9-month project called the "Cutting Edge Audit Office," which aimed to transform how the Wales Audit Office used data and technology. The team consisted of six junior staff that reported directly to the Auditor General (see Box 2.6).

Box 2.6. The Cutting Edge Audit Office Project of the Wales Audit Office

The Cutting Edge Audit Office in Wales was a temporary creation of the Auditor General as a means of transforming the supreme audit institution. Specifically, the office's mandate included the following:

- data acquisition
- data analytics
- the use of data in day-to-day activities
- audit reporting such as data visualisation
- building long-term skills and strategies around audit innovation.

The success of the office was a result of different factors. For instance, by reporting directly to the AG, the Office's work was tangible and left a lasting legacy. The Cutting Edge Audit Office developed and implemented a three year strategic plan on data use, and data was harvested from new sources like the health department and social media. New applications were introduced internally to make work more efficient and relevant including the automation of the analytics process and the adoption of data visualisation as a form of reporting on some audits.

Source: (Auditor General of Wales, 2020[28]).

2.6. Summary of the proposals for action

The ASF's analytics capacity and related processes for data governance are decentralised across different departments. This approach has allowed the ASF to tailor data governance, data management and analytics to suit the needs of individual audit teams. The ASF has developed strong analytic capacities with this approach; however, it has also led to siloes that are exacerbated by insufficient co-ordination. In addition, the ASF has invested in trainings for auditors, but it could take additional steps to understand its priorities for developing digital competencies, including data literacy, so that its auditors can keep pace with the digital change around them in government and society. This includes the need to enhance the ASF's capacity and processes for leveraging analytics to detect integrity risks, as well as the need to further develop a data-centric culture. The following proposals for action are not exhaustive related to improving co-ordination, enhancing analytics for detecting integrity risks, and nurturing a data-centric culture. However, they provide a starting point for the ASF to address key operational challenges and additional considerations for enhancing the use of data and analytics:

- **Strengthen internal co-ordination around data processes and analytics**—Substantive co-ordination on common policies, practices or the development of tools across departments remains limited. Opportunities remain for the ASF to move towards more integrated decision making as a form of internal co-ordination at a departmental and team (i.e. DG) level to provide assurance that there is no duplication or unwanted overlap of efforts. The ASF could conduct a joint review of possible areas of duplicative activities across departments, particularly with respect to its data processing and quality checks, considering the heavy burden these activities put on resources and time. Improved internal co-ordination within the ASF also has the potential to reduce the burden on data owners and auditees to the extent there is a risk that multiple teams within the ASF request the same data.

- **Consider data sharing pilots for breaking down siloes**—To help address internal co-ordination challenges and the potential for inefficiencies, the ASF could conduct a data sharing pilot to address some of the challenges it faces concerning internal (and external) co-ordination, building on precedents for data sharing with other government entities (i.e. SAT, SHCP, and TESOFE). This pilot could involve enhanced communication about similar databases used across departments. If relevant, it could also include sharing responsibilities for data management, cleaning and other common activities that would help to promote efficiencies for resource-intensive tasks and break down or prevent siloes at the auditor level. The pilot could also facilitate the creation of informal channels for auditors to collaborate on data quality issues and methodologies. Conducting a data sharing pilot would help the ASF to identify and then address these challenges constructively and incrementally, using fewer resources to test concepts before the ASF commits to more sustained forms of collaboration.

- **Institutionalise a cross-departmental and cross-functional analytics capacity**—The ASF could take additional steps to institutionalise its analytics capacity. One approach is for the ASF to establish a cross-functional group or community of practice to formalise the current ad hoc communication between teams, and promote consistent exchange of knowledge, expertise and data across departments and DGs. Another model would be for the ASF to create a centralised data service or analytics function that would focus on specific cross-cutting areas of the ASF's analytics processes, while leaving the analysis to the teams and sustaining elements of its current decentralised model. The ASF could also consider establishing a formal role, such as a CDO or CTO, to act as a steward for institution-wide data policies and processes. The precise title and whether this role is fulfilled by one individual or many is less important than further defining and assigning roles and responsibilities for operational data governance, particularly for issues that are institution wide. The ASF can also enhance the cross-functionality of its teams as it further develops its analytics capacity.

- **Conduct an internal assessment to further explore capacity gaps and data capabilities**— While input from ASF officials in the scope of the OECD project established several priorities in terms of improvements to capacities, the ASF could take additional steps to elaborate on this work and identify capacity gaps and needs across a broader group of stakeholders. This could involve an institution-wide assessment of capacity gaps, taking into account data capabilities in relation to defined capabilities and the ASF's plans for future initiatives. As discussed, there are numerous frameworks available to support the ASF in carrying out an assessment of its internal capacity for data and analytics. The assessment should provide a holistic view of gaps and strengths as a basis for refining priorities. The ASF can also benefit from root cause analysis that would provide further insights about the human and cultural elements that influence the ability of the ASF to adopt analytics and fulfil broader goals of digital transformation. As part of this analysis, the ASF could also look at specific challenges facing individual teams and processes, including those related to the application of analytics for detecting irregularities and integrity risks.

- **Improve analysis of risk trends and use of dashboards**—The ASF has established robust processes and capabilities for using data and analytics to detect irregularities. Building on its efforts, the ASF could develop a risk dashboard to improve how it tracks, visualises and communicates risks across the organisation. Developing a dashboard would be a low cost and high return approach to facilitate sharing of risk data and facilitate auditors' analyses of trends and patterns. The risk dashboard can be a vehicle for disseminating such analysis, while improving access to the risk data that the DGAF has to support audits. Moreover, use of dashboards can be useful for continuous monitoring and providing auditors with off-the-shelf or automated tools to conduct analyses and prioritise risks. Visualisations incorporated into dashboards can help auditors to analyse entire datasets for outliers and potential irregularities, allowing more time for analysing information and data and less time collecting it. Visualisations can also help to enhance the readability and impact of the ASF's reporting.

- **Enhance follow-up on findings and create feedback loops to improve analytics**—Follow-up is a fundamental phase of the audit process, reflected in various INTOSAI standards and guidance. ASF institutionalised a follow-up mechanism in the AESII; however, according to officials, the team is under-resourced and follow-up can be lengthy.[8] Knowing the status and the outcome of audits is a critical step in the feedback loop for the DGAF, and other DGs, who rely on the AESII for follow-up. For example, feedback loops—knowing the results of audits and how the DGAF's findings supported outcomes—act as a control for the DGAF's and Forensic Laboratory's own analytics function. The DGAF can fine tune its forensic methodologies and analytics based on the ultimate results of the audits and whether findings led to concrete actions. Optimisation of methodologies helps to reduce false positives and false negatives, and enhance the logic that underlies algorithms and indicators for detecting irregularities.

- **Strengthen analysis of unstructured and semi-structured data**—ASF officials highlighted the need for improving the capacity for managing and analysing unstructured data as one of their top priorities in the coming years. This is in part due to efforts of the AEGF and the AECF to enhance the ASF's architecture, methodologies and tools (e.g. machine learning) to better analyse "big data," which consists of high volumes of unstructured and semi-structured data. The ASF's Digital Mailbox also has the potential to create more unstructured and semi-structured data for the ASF to process. Text mining and other analytic techniques can be helpful to ensure that auditors are not overwhelmed by such data. The ASF can also build on existing capacities for carrying out network analyses, particularly to support the detection of fraud and corruption risks in infrastructure development and public procurement. The diversity of techniques and their underlying tools highlight the need for the ASF to consider strategically how to approach analysis of different types of unstructured and semi-structured data in the future. Defining the process of integrating findings and results from this analysis into the ASF's traditional systems and communication mechanisms, as well as into possible dashboards for auditors to reference, is one critical consideration to ensure that auditors can digest and use the results.

- **Promote digital skills and ethical use of data through trainings**—Introducing new systems, tools or dashboards is necessary, but insufficient, for the ASF to keep pace with the digital change in government and society. The ASF could further develop the skills, motivation and interest in analytic approaches to sustain future analytics initiatives, although it has trained a small number of auditors on big data. This could include, but is not limited to, promoting data literacy as well as developing digital skills, defined as the broader range of abilities to use digital devices, communication applications, and networks to access and manage information. The distinction between data literacy and having digital skills reflects the notion that auditors have different specialities and require varying levels of specialisation when it comes to managing and using data; however, all auditors can benefit from having an understanding and fluency with a range of digital tools and technologies that are critical for the modern auditing profession. Developing digital skills also involves training for auditors to ensure they lead by example as stewards of responsible, accountable and ethical use of data. This would be consistent with ASF's initiative to develop a Policy on Institutional Integrity (*Política de Integridad Institucional*).

- **Create room for experimentation and small wins**—An openness to experimentation is a consistent theme across SAIs that have developed successful analytics initiatives. Even when other aspects of the ASF's work and culture remains risk averse, experimentation creates opportunities for both small wins and small losses. This means a SAI can pilot new methodologies, tools and data sources in a controlled and cost-efficient way before deciding whether to scale up or avoid developing further. Establishing an "Innovation Lab" is one way that SAIs are doing this, which would institutionalise the capacity for experimentation and set the tone for innovation as a strategic objective. However, this is not the only approach for the ASF to consider. The ASF's existing teams demonstrate a high level of ambition to innovate, and there are temporary models, such as project-based initiatives, to tap into the skills and innovative energy of auditors and staff.

References

ACFE (2020), *Report to the Nations: Study on Global Occupational Fraud and Abuse*, https://www.acfe.com/press-release.aspx?id=4295010563#:~:text=In%20the%20ACFE%27s%202020%20Report,loss%20of%20%248%2C300%20a%20month. [1]

ASF (2021), *Avances en la implementación de nuevas herramientas tecnológicas aplicadas a la fiscalización superior*. [2]

Auditor General of Wales (2020), *Cutting Edge Audit Office*, https://www.eurorai.org/public/Attachment/2020/6/Sevilla-presentationSLISLE.pdf. [28]

Auditor General South Africa (2020), *Consolidated General Report on National and Provincial Audit Outcomes*, https://www.agsa.co.za/Portals/0/Reports/PFMA/201920/PFMA%202019-20%20Report%20-%20signed.pdf. [15]

Baesens, B., V. Van Vlasselaer and W. Verbeke (2015), "Using Descriptive, Predictive, and Social Network Technique: A guide to Data Science for Fraud Detection", *John Wiley & Sons, Inc.*. [5]

Canadian Audit and Accountability Foundation (2020), *Better Integrating Root Cause Analysis into Public sector performance auditing*, https://www.caaf-fcar.ca/images/pdfs/research-publications/RootCauseAnalysisEN.pdf. [16]

Commonwealth Fraud Prevention Centre, Government of Australia (2020), *Data Sharing Pilots, Leading Practice Guide*, https://www.counterfraud.gov.au/sites/default/files/2021-02/data-sharing-pilots-leading-practice-guide.pdf (accessed on 3 August 2021). [6]

Dickson, M. and P. Asagba (2020), "The Semi-Structured Data Model and Implementation Issues for Semi-Structured Data", *International Journal of Innovation and Sustainability*, Vol. 3/2020, pp. 47-51, https://papers.ssrn.com/sol3/papers.cfm?abstract_id=3726802. [29]

EUROSAI (2021), *GERMANY: Using text mining methods to analyse public communication of our auditees*, https://eurosai-it.org/news/newsletter/1-2021/updates-from-itwg-members/germnay-using-text-mining-methods-to-analyse-public-communication-of-our-auditees. [20]

EUROSAI (2019), *Follow-up of the Implementation of records*, https://www.eurosai.org/handle404?exporturi=/export/sites/eurosai/.content/documents/2021-02-03-Final-report-for-EUROSAI.pdf. [18]

Government of Mexico (2021), "Diario Oficial de la Federación", in *Agreement amending, adding and repealing several provisions of the Internal Regulations of the Superior Audit Office of the Federation*. [34]

Government of New Zealand (2021), *Operational data governance*, https://www.data.govt.nz/toolkit/data-governance/odgf/. [30]

Government of New Zealand (2020), *The Data Capability Framework (DCF) Guide*, https://www.data.govt.nz/assets/Uploads/Training/Data-Capability-Framework/Data-Capability-Framework-Guide.pdf. [14]

House of Commons, United Kingdom (2017), *Value for Money Study, Delivery of Benefits From the NAO's IT Enabled Change Program*, https://www.parliament.uk/globalassets/documents/public-accounts-commission/15-NAO-VFM-report-on-IT-enabled-change-programme.pdf. [8]

INTOSAI (2020), *Strategic Management Handbook for Supreme Audit Institutions*, https://www.idi.no/elibrary/well-governed-sais/strategy-performance-measurement-reporting/1139-sai-strategic-management-handbook-version-1/file. [13]

INTOSAI (2019), *INTOSAI-P - 12 - The Value and Benefits of Supreme Audit Institutions – making a difference to the lives of citizens*, https://www.issai.org/pronouncements/intosai-p-12-the-value-and-benefits-of-supreme-audit-institutions-making-a-difference-to-the-lives-of-citizens/. [31]

INTOSAI (2015), *GUID - 9030 - Good Practices Related to SAI Independence*, https://www.issai.org/pronouncements/guid-9030-good-practices-related-to-sai-independence/. [32]

Kärki, M. and M. Saarteinen (2020), *National Audit Office of Finland: Strategy and practice when using data in auditing and monitoring*, Presentation at OECD Workshop (18 November 2020). [23]

National Banking and Stock Commission, Government of Mexico (2016), *Development Bank (BD)*, https://www.gob.mx/cnbv/acciones-y-programas/banca-de-desarrollo-bd. [33]

OAGN Innovation Lab (2020), *Data Science & Machine Learning*, https://www.intosaipas.org/wp-content/uploads/2020/02/Agenda-item-1H_2019_Data-Science-PASmeeting-1.pdf (accessed on 3 September 2021). [27]

OECD (2020), "Building digital workforce capacity and skills for data-intensive science", *OECD Science, Technology and Industry Policy Papers*, No. 90, OECD Publishing, Paris, https://doi.org/10.1787/e08aa3bb-en. [25]

OECD (2020), *Digital Government in Mexico: Sustainable and Inclusive Transformation*, OECD Digital Government Studies, OECD Publishing, Paris, https://doi.org/10.1787/6db24495-en. [9]

OECD (2020), *Good Practice Principles for Data Ethics in the Public Sector*, OECD, Paris, https://www.oecd.org/gov/digital-government/good-practice-principles-for-data-ethics-in-the-public-sector.pdf. [24]

OECD (2019), *Analytics for Integrity: Data-Driven Approaches for Enhancing Corruption and Fraud Risk Assessments*, OECD, Paris, https://www.oecd.org/gov/ethics/analytics-for-integrity.pdf. [21]

Office of the Auditor General of Norway (2021), *Introduction to Text Mining for Auditors*, https://idi.no/elibrary/relevant-sais/sai-innovations/innovative-sais-going-f-a-r/1285-marketplace-introduction-to-text-mining-for-auditors-office-of-the-auditor-general-of-norway/file. [26]

Office of the Comptroller and Auditor General of India (2017), *Guidelines on Data Analogue*, https://cag.gov.in/uploads/guidelines/Guidelines-on-Data-Analytics-book-05de4f7fd52e565-67820093.pdf. [11]

Onwujekwe, G., N. Ngwum and K. Osei-Bryson (2020), *A Framework for Capturing and Analyzing Unstructured and Semi-structured Data for a Knowledge Management System*. [22]

Special Audit of Financial Compliance, ASF (2021), *Sistema de Inteligencia para la Fiscalización Superior de la AECF*, [PowerPoint Slides].   [3]

Stockpoll, B. (2021), *Making the business case for a chief data officer*, https://mitsloan.mit.edu/ideas-made-to-matter/making-business-case-a-chief-data-officer.   [10]

Strimling, A. (2006), "Stepping Out of the Tracks: Cooperation Between Official Diplomats and Private Facilitators", *International Negotiation*, Vol. 2006/11, pp. 91-127, https://brill.com/view/journals/iner/11/1/article-p91_5.xml?language=en.   [4]

Talib, R. et al. (2016), "Text Mining: Techniques, Applications and Issues", *International Journal of Advanced Computer Science and Applications*, Vol. 7/11, pp. 414-418, https://thesai.org/Downloads/Volume7No11/Paper_53-Text_Mining_Techniques_Applications_and_Issues.pdf.   [19]

The European Court of Auditors (2019), "Developing data services for audit", *Presentation of Magdalena Cordero, Director of Information, Workplace and Innovation*, https://ecademy.eca.europa.eu/pluginfile.php/260/mod_resource/content/1/Developing%20data%20services%20for%20auditors%20%E2%80%93%20the%20ECA%20experience.pdf (accessed on 3 August 20021).   [12]

UK National Audit Office (2019), *Transparency Report*, https://www.nao.org.uk/wp-content/uploads/2020/07/National-Audit-Office-Transparency-Report-2019-20.pdf.   [7]

UK National Audit Office (2018), *Data Analytics at the National Audit Office (UK)*, https://www.intosaipas.org/wp-content/uploads/2020/02/Agenda-item_2A_Andy-Fisher_Data-Analytics-at-the-UK-NAO.pdf (accessed on 3 August 2021).   [17]

Notes

[1] Development banking institutions are entities of the Federal Public Administration, with their own legal personality and assets, constituted as national credit companies. Their main objective is to facilitate access to savings and financing for individuals and companies, as well as to provide them with technical assistance and training (National Banking and Stock Commission, Government of Mexico, 2016[33]).

[2] See articles 9, 17, section XI, and 23 of the Law on Auditing and Accountability of the Federation (*Ley de Fiscalización y Rendición de Cuentas de la Federación*, LFRCF), and 5 section XI, of the Internal Regulations of the Superior Audit Office of the Federation (*Reglamento Interior de la Auditoría Superior de la Federación*).

[3] As introduced in Chapter 1, this references the New Zealand government's approach to data governance which makes a distinction between political governance and operational data governance. The latter is associated with data activities and needs at the operational level of an organisation (Government of New Zealand, 2021[30]).

[4] See, for instance, https://idi.no/elibrary/professional-sais/issai-implementation-handbooks/handbooks-english.

[5] The AESII was recently restructured in the amendment to the ASF's internal regulations in August 2021 (Government of Mexico, 2021[34]).

[6] For instance, see INTOSAI-P 12 The Value and Benefits of SAIs – making a difference to the lives of citizens (INTOSAI, 2019[31]) and INTOSAI GUID 9030: Good Practices Related to SAI Independence (INTOSAI, 2015[32]).

[7] Semi-structured data has defining or consistent characteristics, but it does not have the structure of a relational database. For instance, emails have unstructured content with a predictable structure with common fields like sender, recipient, subject and time stamps. Much of what people classify as unstructured data is actually semi-structured due to classifying characteristics of the data (Dickson and Asagba, 2020[29]).

[8] As noted, the AESII underwent a restructuring following the amendment to the ASF's internal regulation, which occurred after the completion of the analysis for this report.

www.ingramcontent.com/pod-product-compliance
Lightning Source LLC
LaVergne TN
LVHW080613200726
843509LV00007B/296